BOOMTOWN LANDMARKS

BOOMTOWN LANDMARKS

edited by **Laurie Hertzel**

Illustrations by Kathryn Marsaa

Pfeifer-Hamilton
Duluth, Minnesota

Pfeifer-Hamilton Publishers
210 West Michigan
Duluth MN 55802-1908
218-727-0500

Boomtown Landmarks

Printed in the United States of America by Arcata Graphics company.
10   9   8   7   6   5   4   3   2   1

Editorial Director: Susan Gustafson
Manuscript Editor: Patrick Gross
Art Director: Joy Morgan Dey
Cartographer: Paul Hapy

Library of Congress Catalog Card Number
93-84406

ISBN 0-938586-50-5

Publisher's Foreword

In 1985 we established Pfeifer-Hamilton with a mission—creating quality gift books that celebrate the special beauty and unique lifestyle of the North Country. Amazingly, however, until now we just never quite got around to publishing a book on Duluth—our adopted hometown, and the city we have grown to love.

We take pride in the publication of *Boomtown Landmarks,* researched by Steve Boman and edited by Laurie Hertzel, the first in this new *Discover Duluth* series. Each year we plan to add another volume that will celebrate the many faces and rich heritage of Duluth.

To those who built our city,
and those who held on through the tough times,
to those who strive to preserve its past,
and those who invest in its future,
to all those who love Duluth as we do,
we hope this book helps you
rediscover Duluth.

Donald A Tubesing   Nancy Loving Tubesing
Publishers
May 1993

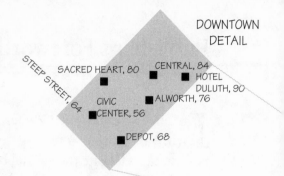

DOWNTOWN
DETAIL

STEEP STREET, 64

SACRED HEART, 80   CENTRAL, 84

HOTEL
DULUTH, 90

CIVIC   ALWORTH, 76
CENTER, 56

DEPOT, 68

The Landmarks

This map will help you find the
Boomtown Landmarks as you
explore Duluth. The number after each place name refers to the
page in this book that describes
the landmark.

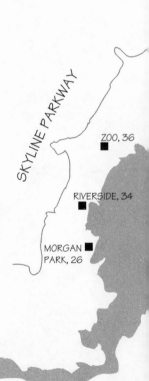

SKYLINE PARKWAY

ZOO, 36

RIVERSIDE, 34

MORGAN
PARK, 26

FOND DU LAC, 20

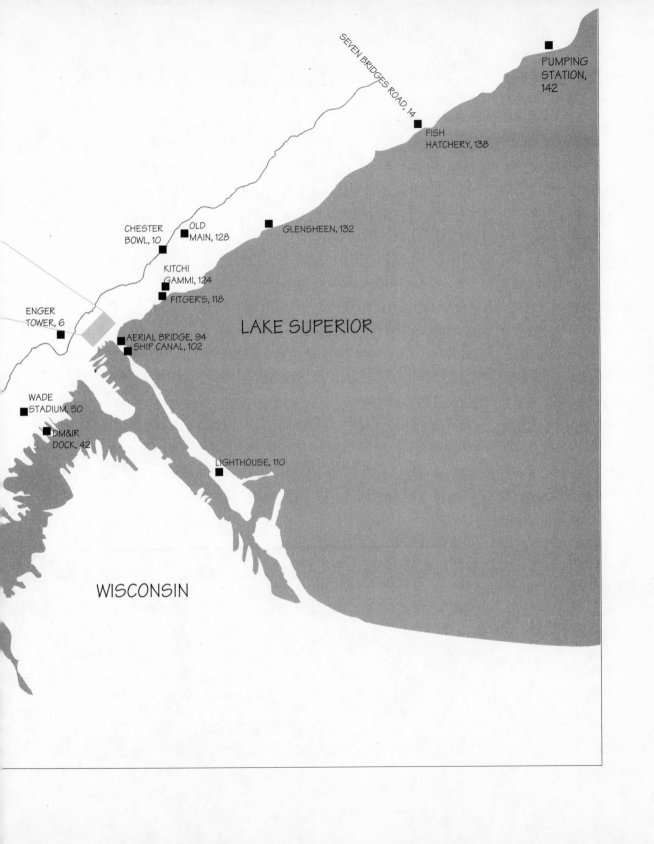

PUMPING
STATION,
142

SEVEN BRIDGES ROAD, 14

FISH
HATCHERY, 138

CHESTER
BOWL, 10

OLD
MAIN, 128

GLENSHEEN, 132

KITCHI
GAMMI, 124

FITGER'S, 118

ENGER
TOWER, 6

LAKE SUPERIOR

AERIAL BRIDGE, 94
SHIP CANAL, 102

WADE
STADIUM, 50

DM&IR
DOCK, 42

LIGHTHOUSE, 110

WISCONSIN

Acknowledgments

Thanks to Todd White for years of friendship, encouragement, and no MSG. And thanks, as always, to Don and Nancy Tubesing, Susan Gustafson, and the others at Pfeifer-Hamilton who gave me the reason and the impetus to stop and think about what it is I love about Duluth. And special thanks to the *Duluth News-Tribune,* for allowing me time away from my regular duties to write it all down.

—Laurie Hertzel
May, 1993

The Neighborhoods

WOODLAND

KENWOOD   HUNTERS PARK

LESTER PARK

LAKESIDE

CHESTER PARK

CONGDON

DULUTH HEIGHTS   EAST END

CENTRAL
HILLSIDE

LAKE SUPERIOR

PIEDMONT

WEST END

BAYVIEW HEIGHTS

PARK POINT

WEST DULUTH

SPIRIT VALLEY

SMITHVILLE   RIVERSIDE

MORGAN
PARK

WISCONSIN

GARY

NEW DULUTH

FOND DU LAC

Introduction

Something about Duluth gets under a person's skin. It could be its incredible natural beauty, trapped as the city is between the mammoth blue lake and the steep green and granite hills. Or it could be its unusual past, the fact that it began as an Indian village and eventually grew into a busy and important seaport, with ships from all over the world calling at its docks to load up on iron ore and steel and timber and grain.

Perhaps it is the lake itself, the largest freshwater lake in the world and the feature that most defines Duluth. Every day the lake influences the weather, the economy, and the mood of the city. Large ships have broken up and been swallowed by Lake Superior when the weather turned violent; tourists fish and sail and swim in the lake when it is sparkling and calm.

Or perhaps it's the city's clearly defined neighborhoods, each almost a proud little town in itself, from the self-contained westernmost neighborhood of Fond du Lac, an old fur trading post and Indian village, to the sedate eastern neighborhood of Lester Park, where bears and moose still occasionally wander into yards from the North Shore forests.

Or perhaps it's the city's tenacity. Duluth has been a boomtown, and it has been a bust-town. It survived the panic of 1857, when everyone was sure the town would fold. The population swelled again in the early 1900s to more than one hundred thousand, when Duluth was proclaimed to be the next Chicago or Pittsburgh. It shrank again during the Great Depression.

Most recently, the city clawed its way up from near bottom after a series of plant closings forced hundreds of people out of work and out of town in the 1970s and 1980s. Today, Duluth is a solid city of about eighty-two thousand people, with an economy dependent on tourism, education, and a booming medical business.

Like any city, Duluth can be defined in

many ways. It is a city of woods and ravines and rocks and water, a place where people live close to nature, a place where deer and raccoons and bears and the occasional moose wander into backyards and down streets and cause not as much surprise or havoc as you might expect.

It is also a city of culture and education, with a ballet and a symphony, a dozen museums, half that many theater companies, hundreds of writers and musicians, two colleges, and a university.

It is a hard-working city, a city with strong muscles and a weathered face and a collar as blue as the sky.

Duluth is also a city of buildings, a city where the marks its men and women made are still visible. The city's fascinating past, shows in its landmarks, which—unlike those in many large cities—still stand, well preserved.

Boomtown Duluth's lumber barons and mining barons and shipbuilders built elaborate homes in eastern Duluth and got factories and docks running in western Duluth. Thousands of immigrants from Scandinavia and Eastern Europe came, too,

Rising from depression

In the summer of 1891, Duluth needed some good news. Bank failures across the country had triggered an economic depression, hundreds of Duluthians had fallen seriously ill because of unsanitary drinking water, and the city administration was embroiled in annexation battles. ■ A front page advertisement in the *Duluth Daily Tribune* advised city residents to look to the lessons taught by General Ulysses S. Grant during the Civil War: "We should all learn that in the face of difficulties and discouragements the best way is to hold our ground and never falter." ■ The paid message from a Duluth realtor then recommended that readers "call and we will show you some good stuff to buy."

and built homes and churches, making their distinct mark in some of the Finntown and Italian and Serbo-Croation neighborhoods—still well defined.

This book is only an introduction to Duluth. It's not a history, though you'll find a smattering of historical information. It's not a guidebook, though it tells you about places to go. It's not a tourism manual, though visitors certainly will find it useful.

The book begins with a quick west to east trip along Skyline Parkway. This journey, with its stop at Enger Tower, will give you an overview of the city and harbor.

Return to the west, following Interstate 35 and Highway 23, and begin your trip east again as the book takes you logically through the city along the waterfront, from the westernmost tip of Fond du Lac straight through to the eastern edge.

You'll visit a variety of landmarks, from the taconite docks to the old churches, from the office building that was once the tallest building in the state to beautiful Glensheen mansion.

But keep in mind, as you read, that this book is only a guide. Bring along your own special interests and viewpoint. As you stop at the Riverside Marina or Enger Tower or the old lighthouse down on Park Point, take your time. Look around. Duluth offers a lot more out there, waiting to be explored in its neighborhoods and side streets.

Contents

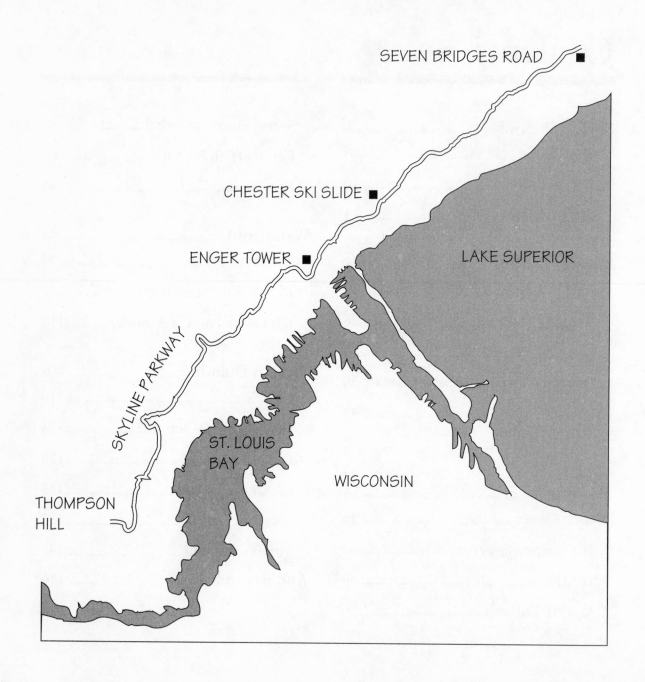

SEVEN BRIDGES ROAD ■

CHESTER SKI SLIDE ■

ENGER TOWER ■

LAKE SUPERIOR

SKYLINE PARKWAY

ST. LOUIS
BAY

WISCONSIN

THOMPSON
HILL

Skyline Parkway

Duluth was built in a valley; the town stretches along the rocky, sandy shore of Lake Superior and climbs halfway up the steep and rugged hill behind. Close to the top of the hill a road traverses the city, from west to east. From this road, Skyline Parkway, you can get an overall feel for the town. Its vistas give you a place to step back, get perspective on the geography, and size up Duluth.

Skyline Parkway begins at the Thompson Hill Information Center, on the western edge of the city just off Interstate 35. It ends by the Lester River, near the eastern boundary. In between, it takes you past many of the more famous landmarks of Duluth—Spirit Mountain, Enger Tower, Chester Bowl.

In most places Skyline is a narrow, twisting road, built at times frighteningly close to the edge of the cliff. But you'll find places to pull over and get off your bicycle or out of your car and just LOOK. From almost anywhere on top of the hill you get a sweeping view of Duluth.

Skyline Parkway begins and ends in near-wilderness. At its western edge, by Spirit Mountain, you can find trilliums growing in the springtime—great white triangular blossoms that look, from the

Thompson Hill Information Center

Skyline Parkway begins on Thompson Hill, and although the modern glass-fronted Thompson Hill Information Center is not a boomtown landmark, it provides an excellent place to begin your trip. Looking down from six hundred feet above Lake Superior, the view of the St. Louis River is marvelous, and binoculars are available to bring the details up close. ■ Here you can pick up maps and information about Duluth attractions.

Duluth by night

Stars twinkling above you, lamplight warm in the windows of hillside homes, brilliant bridge and street lights reflected in the harbor—on a clear night, the view from Skyline Parkway is breathtaking. ■ **Even Duluthians, returning from hurried business trips, cannot help but be awed by their beautiful city as they wind their way down Thompson Hill.**

road, like scraps of paper scattered across the forest floor. Here, too, you can often find deer, shy and big-eyed, grazing along the roadside.

At the city's eastern border, Skyline passes by a rushing creek and Hawk Ridge nature preserve. It finally disappears in the depths of the Lester Park woods.

But Skyline has its urban elements, too. From various vantage points, such as at Enger Tower, you can look out over the bustling waterfront, the busy docks, the grain elevators, and the Aerial Bridge, which spends most of the summer first rising to let boats through and then descending to let passengers across and then rising again.

So take a ride along the Skyline. And be prepared for the best views in town.

Where did this hole come from?

As you look down at Lake Superior from Skyline Parkway, six hundred feet above the lake, you may ask yourself how this gigantic freshwater lake was created deep in the heart of the continent. ■ It all began with a shift in the earth's crust, one billion two hundred million years ago. Through that fracture molten lava flowed out across the surface. As layers of lava accumulated, becoming five miles thick in some areas, it formed Duluth's bedrock, called gabbro. ■ The weight of the lava depressed the crust of the earth. Shallow seas formed, then retreated, leaving behind soft sedimentary rocks such as sandstone. ■ During the Pleistocene Ice Age, which began about a million years ago, great sheets of ice covered the continent as far south as Kansas. As the climate warmed and cooled, glaciers advanced and retreated, each time gouging the land, scraping out vast cavities and smaller depressions. ■ When you stand on Skyline Parkway, you are standing at the water level of Glacial Lake Duluth, the body of water formed when the last glacier receded almost twelve thousand years ago. Two thousand years later, the water level had dropped 225 feet. Precipitation and glacial meltwater have brought it to its current level of 600 feet above sea level. ■ As you tour the city and the area, look for evidence of this geologic activity, gabbro cliffs on the north shore of the lake, clay banks on the south, sandstone deposits and the fine sand of Park Point that has eroded from them.

Enger Tower

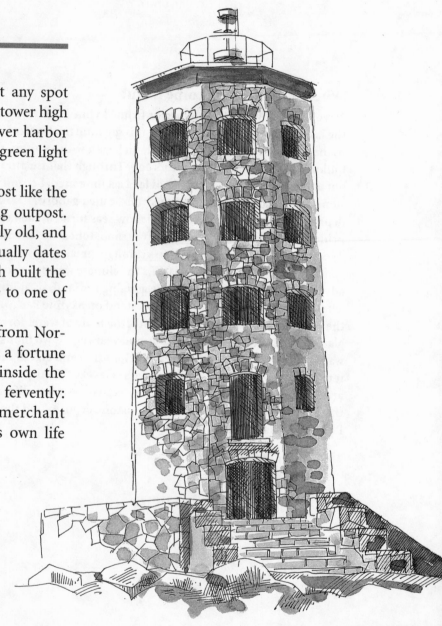

You can see it from almost any spot along the freeway—a stone tower high on the hilltop. It looks down over harbor and city, illuminated by a single green light on top.

From a distance, it looks almost like the ancient remains of some Viking outpost. But Enger Tower isn't particularly old, and it has no warrior history. It actually dates back only to 1939, when Duluth built the octagonal structure as a tribute to one of its adopted sons.

Bert Enger came to Duluth from Norway as a young man and made a fortune in business. A bronze plaque inside the tower tells his story briefly and fervently: "From common laborer to merchant prince, he demonstrated in his own life

The best view in town
A winding staircase leads to the top of Enger Tower, where you will enjoy a panoramic view of Duluth and the harbor.

As you approach Enger Tower from the west, follow the left fork where the road divides to circle the hill. Then turn right on the steep road leading to the park.

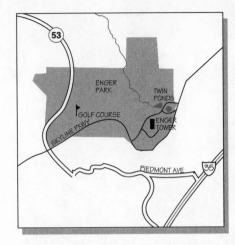

that America is a land of opportunity for the immigrant and that her civilization is enriched by his citizenship."

More influential than the enrichment of his citizenship, of course, were Enger's donating a large section of hilltop land to the city and his leaving two-thirds of his estate to Duluth. That generosity compelled the city to build the tower in his memory.

You get to Enger Park from Skyline Parkway, Duluth's west-to-east hillside drive. The park is along the western half, at about Fourteenth Avenue West. Signs will show you the way. From the parking lot, a rocky pathway leads to the tower. You can climb to the top up a winding staircase and look out through square windows at each landing. Inside, the monument is a bit dismal, scrawled with graffiti and dark. But once you get to the top, it's always exhilarating—brisk and windy no matter what time of year, offering the most dramatic view in town.

Bring your binoculars. From Enger, you can look out over most of the city, as far

Wedding flowers
The Enger Park gardens, in a riot of color, provide a beautiful setting for summer weddings.

west as Morgan Park and nearly as far as Canada in the other direction. You can see the factories and the grain elevators and the Aerial Bridge, the harbor and downtown and Park Point, the pleasure boats bobbing in the lake and the oceangoing ships gliding by. No other spot gives you quite as sweeping an overview of the town.

The tower sits in the middle of Enger Park, surrounded by paved walkways, lush gardens, crushed limestone hiking trails through the woods, and a stone picnic pavilion. The many flower beds, brilliant with

Go Golfing

Enger Park Golf Course, a twenty-seven-hole hilltop golf course, is just down the road from Enger Park. The course has been carved out of the woods, and it's not uncommon to see deer, red fox, or raccoons wander onto it. ■ The view from many tees is captivating. It looks as if you could hit your drive into the harbor a few miles away. Alas, because of the temptation to try, many first-timers dub their shot into the woods.

color in the summer, along with the frilly wooden gazebo, give the park a civilized air. People get married here, or come here for family reunions, or just sit and daydream in quiet reflection.

From the foot of the tower you can hike into the woods, where it is still and quiet, and where you might very well spook a deer or a coyote. In the fall, you'll see evidence of bears, though it's fairly unusual to actually see one, since they mostly cruise through at night.

Or you can climb out onto the steep rocky cliffs, overgrown with sumac and scrubby pines. It's often breezy here, but you can soak up the sun on large, flat rocks, pick berries, and, of course, enjoy the view.

The Twin Ports

From Enger Tower you can see across the bay to Superior, Wisconsin, Duluth's twin port. The cityscapes are quite different—Duluth clinging precariously to its hillside, Superior planted firmly on prairie-flat ground. However, the industrial base of each city is similar. Superior's waterfront is also bordered by grain elevators and ore docks. ■ Barker's Island shelters a lovely marina with slips for four hundred pleasure boats. ■ Fairlawn Mansion, a Victorian mansion built in 1890 for Martin Pattison, a lumber baron and a miner, faces Barker's Island across Highway 2. The forty-two-room mansion is open daily to the public, year-round. The mansion also houses a collection of David F. Barry photographs and Native American artifacts.

Take a swim

Just east of Enger, you'll cross a stone bridge between two small lakes, known as Twin Ponds. The first is a secluded and beautiful old swimming hole with steep, grassy banks for sunbathing and a small grove of birch trees for shade. The second, across the road, is still stocked with fish for the underage angler.

Chester Bowl

In a town of hills and snow, a town populated by Scandinavians, it comes as no surprise that skiing is one of the most popular wintertime sports. All kinds of skiing—downhill, cross-country, and, of course, ski jumping.

Chester Bowl, the park at Eighteenth Avenue East along Skyline Parkway, has long

To those who have never experienced the joy of flying through the air on a pair of skis, Big Chester appears terrifyingly high—even from a distance.

10

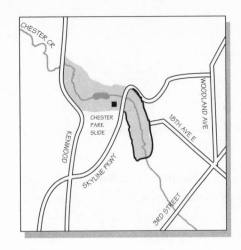

Skyline Parkway crosses Chester Bowl at Eighteenth Avenue East.

been one of the most popular ski jumping sites in the area. Its tallest jump—Big Chester—looms high above the treetops of the park and is visible from all directions. Its metal scaffolding rises 115 feet high; the jump itself is a 45-meter slide.

The Duluth Ski Club has been around since 1905, when a group of Scandinavians got together to make their sport official. The very next year, Duluthian Ole Feiring brought home the United States national jumping championship. And Duluthians have been winning awards—in everything from local contests to the Olympics—ever since.

Spirit Mountain

Chester Bowl offers skiing for the brave—most recreational skiers will never dare descend Big Chester. Several other kinds of skiing, however, are available at Chester Bowl and throughout the city. Cross-country trails traverse parks and forests, and at the western end of town, Spirit

In the early twenties, "Spot," mascot of the Duluth Ski Club, was a feature in tournaments. Using a special pair of skis, Spot rode the landings of hills in northern Minnesota. Records show he never spilled on the downhill runs.

11

Mountain Recreation Area, which opened in 1974, provides downhill skiing among the best in the Midwest.

Its twenty runs, for beginners as well as advanced skiers, are served by five chair lifts. The longest run, 5,400 feet, has a vertical drop of 700 feet. It may not be Aspen but it can still be exciting. If you're not ready for a mile-long ride, instructors are available on the beginner hills.

Duluth is a snowy city but Spirit Mountain does not depend entirely on naturally occurring snow. To keep the runs open and in good condition from Thanksgiving through late March, groomers make snow whenever nature does not cooperate.

A safe sport

Duluth has hosted a handful of ski jumping championships. National competitions were held here in 1908, 1915, 1926, 1942, and 1950. Thousands of spectators turned out for these events—more than forty-two thousand came to the 1942 competition, held at Fond du Lac. ■ Over the years, ski jumping has changed dramatically. In 1942, the longest jump was 194 feet. Today, with faster skis, larger jumps, and more aerodynamic clothing, ski jumpers have flown nearly 600 feet—although not in Duluth! ■ The consensus is, however, that early jumping was more risky than ski jumping today. In the past, ski jumps curved up at the end, actually shooting the jumper up into the air. Modern jumps don't have this lip, so while flyers go much farther down the hill, they are never as far off the ground.

Seven Bridges Road

Seven Bridges Road runs steep and winding for nearly two miles from Hawk Ridge down to Superior Street. You won't find that name on a map or on street signs, though, the official name is Occidental Boulevard. But you'll be hard pressed to find a Duluthian who calls it that. Instead, it is known for the seven lovely stone bridges, built of native Duluth bluestone back in the 1930s by Works Progress Administration workers.

Since Seven Bridges Road can be a little difficult to find off Skyline Parkway, you may want to begin your drive near the

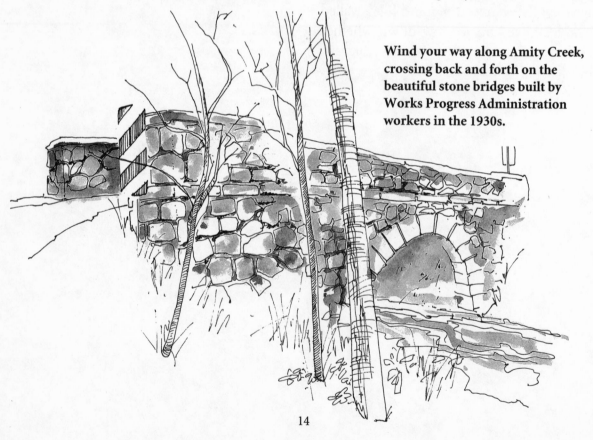

Wind your way along Amity Creek, crossing back and forth on the beautiful stone bridges built by Works Progress Administration workers in the 1930s.

Skyline Parkway, though a bit hard to follow in its easternmost reaches, will lead you to Seven Bridges Road.

lake just east of Sixtieth Avenue East. The road hugs and crisscrosses Amity creek all the way up. You'll see a few houses at the foot of the road—lucky people, to live in such a beautiful spot—but once you cross the first bridge you seem to leave the city behind. You can't take Seven Bridges Road quickly; the sharp curves and high-walled bridges force you to slow down whether you're in a car, on foot or on a bicycle. Enjoy the view of Lester Park on the right side of the road, a large, hilly, wooded park with hiking paths and lighted cross-country ski trails.

About a mile up, the road winds past a high steep hill used in the winter by sledders and inner-tube riders. In the summer, the hill is green and fragrant, covered with soft grass, buttercups, and daisies.

After another mile or so, Seven Bridges Road ends. It splits, actually, into two roads. To the right, it heads to other roads in rural Duluth, where people live in big houses with large yards. To the left, it becomes Hawk Ridge, a two-mile gravel

Miles of groomed cross-country ski trails traverse city parks. Ski them in winter. Hike them in summer.

stretch back toward town that hugs the cliff and offers more spectacular views of the lake.

Hawk Ridge

Every fall people come from all over the world to stand on this breezy bluff and stare at the sky. Binoculars in hand, they crane their necks and scan the sky above—and sometimes below—for the beating wings of migrating hawks.

Hawk Ridge, a two-mile-long gravel road that links Seven Bridges Road with Glenwood Avenue, is the farthest east extension of the Skyline Parkway. It makes an excellent vantage point from which to watch one of the most spectacular hawk migrations in the world.

Every year, hawks and other raptors head south along a natural route known as the Mississippi Flyway. When they hit Lake Superior, though, they change course because they won't fly over such a vast expanse of open water. Instead, the birds funnel down along the lakeshore, which brings them past Hawk Ridge.

The migrating birds start showing up in great numbers in September and October. Though the ridge is most famous for the migration of hawks, eagles, and falcons, every fall thousands of other land and shore birds pass by this bluff. Later in the year, it's a great spot to watch all kinds of owls.

So every autumn, as the leaves turn bright and the air grows crisp, birders show up here to set up their chairs and spotting scopes and spend entire days counting the migrating hawks and keeping an eye out for exotic or rare birds that somehow got swept up in the annual massive flight.

It's a beautiful spot to visit, whether or not you're a birder. If you look up, you see the sky, dotted with hawks. If you look down, far below you see the neat rooftops of the orderly and quiet Lakeside neighborhood.

Farther out is the shimmering blue of Lake Superior. And behind you in dense woods a maze of hiking trails cut through the bright sumac and golden aspen and tall, windy pines. A perfect spot to rest your tired neck, stretch your legs, and enjoy the fall.

■　■　■

You've completed your journey along Duluth's high ground. Now, for a chance to explore the city from the inside, drop down to lake level and return to the west, crossing the city on the most modern and efficient pathway—Interstate 35. It will carry you through the heart of town in just a few minutes. Exit at Central Avenue and take Highway 23 on out to Fond du Lac.

The fast lane

Interstate 35—the longest stretch of freeway in the country—begins in Duluth and ends in Laredo, Texas. The Duluth extension includes a lighted, tiled tunnel that brings the freeway underground and keeps it discreet as it passes through Duluth's "Historic District" near Fitger's Brewery and the Kitchi Gammi Club. ■ Along London Road, several cagelike pedestrian bridges have been built—modern sculptures, almost—that take people over the busy freeway and down to the quiet rocks of Lake Superior below. ■ Closer to downtown, a large park sits atop the freeway, planted with grass, trees, and shrubs, making a natural sound barrier. The park stretches between Fitger's and Canal Park, linking the two tourist areas and providing green space downtown. ■ From this surprisingly quiet area you can look down on the Lakewalk and watch the joggers and bicyclists. You can look out on the lake and watch the waves crashing against the rocks—or, on calm summer days, wave at the sailboats as they bob past.

DM&IR
DOCKS

WADE
STADIUM

LAKE SUPERIOR
ZOO

RIVERSIDE

MORGAN
PARK

WISCONSIN

FOND DU LAC

Western Duluth

The western half of the city is the lungs and muscle of Duluth. Here Duluth began, three hundred years ago, as an Indian village. Here are the factories, and the ore docks, and the grain elevators, and the ethnic pockets where many of the children and grandchildren of the first immigrants still live.

In the western half you'll find big sprawling family homes with vegetable gardens and bird feeders in the yards, the ghostly remains of the old U.S. Steel plant, and the empty lot where the cement factory once stood.

Here, too, you will find beautiful old churches, like St. George Serbian Orthodox Church, and community centers where neighbors have gathered for generations. Here's the Italian-American Club, and the Goodfellowship Club, which began as a private club for the employees of U.S. Steel.

Don't call this West Duluth; the city is made up of more than twenty neighborhoods, each with a strong identity and a fierce loyalty to its own name and boundaries. West Duluth is just one of the many distinct neighborhoods sprinkled between Fond du Lac and downtown.

As you cruise through the western neighborhoods, you'll find fishing docks and well-trod hiking trails along the sparkling St. Louis River; you'll pass the old Duluth Zoo, slowly being modernized but preserving its past in the beautiful and sturdy WPA-era stone buildings.

Of course the western neighborhoods offer much more than you will find in these pages. Follow the guide, but veer off along the way and explore on your own. Discover some of the parks, like Lincoln Park with its rocky gorge and stone pavilion. Or wander the main streets of downtown West Duluth, with its interesting shops and neighborhood bakeries.

And while you are here, bask in the friendliness that typifies western Duluth.

Fond du Lac

Along, narrow city, Duluth stretches like a 23-mile ribbon along the shore of Lake Superior. The westernmost tip of this ribbon is the neighborhood of Fond du Lac, French for "head of the lake."

It was originally an Ojibwa village. The nearby St. Louis River was an important waterway for the Ojibwa; it feeds into Lake Superior to the east, and to the west it could get them, eventually, to the Upper Mississippi River.

The first white man happened by in 1679. He was Daniel Greysolon, Sieur du Lhut, the explorer for whom Duluth is

Built in 1867, a modest frame home in Fond du Lac is Duluth's oldest residence.

A drive along Highway 23 (Grand Avenue) will take you through several western neighborhoods, including Fond du Lac.

---

named. He came to the area to meet with the Indians and persuade them to do their fur trading with the French, rather than the British. For various reasons, almost one hundred years passed before the white men came back, ready to build their wooden houses and claim the area for their own. British fur traders came in the late 1700s, and John Jacob Astor established his American Fur Company trading post in Fond du Lac in 1817.

Tucked down a side street of Fond du Lac (along 133rd Avenue West, just off

Sieur du Lhut

Duluth is named after Daniel Greysolon Sieur du Lhut, Gendarme de la Garde du Roi. He grew up near the city of Lyon, France, then moved to Montreal. Some biographers believe that his explorations were a tonic for a broken heart. ■ On the eastern end of Duluth, in Ordean Court on the UMD campus, you can see the statue of Sieur du Lhut sculpted by Jacques Lipchitz. ■ Dulhut, du Lud, du Lude, du Luht and Duluth—both the spelling and the pronunciation have changed over the years.

21

Paddle a canoe

Fond du Lac is one of Duluth's most rugged and pristine neighborhoods. You can slip a canoe into the calm waters of the St. Louis River from just about any spot along the low-lying banks. ■ **Chamber's Grove park, just half a block down Highway 23 from the last house is one good place to begin your paddle. From there you can float down the river to some of the lovely little islands—Amik, Nekuk, Wahbegor, and Ondaig. It's about a five-mile paddle to the Highway 39 bridge, and just beyond that lies Spirit Lake.** ■ **The St. Louis River offers good fishing, but unfortunately years of pollution and contamination have made the fish dangerous to eat in large quantities. You might want to practice catch-and-release here, or better yet, just glide by and watch nature—the herons and eagles and mallards and beavers and otters—but leave it undisturbed.**

Highway 23), a modest wooden sign says "Historic Site." The bronze plaque imbedded in stone tells passersby about the Ojibwa village and du Lhut's arrival here three hundred years ago.

From this spot you can see the river, calm and wide, flowing gently around the bend. It is shaded by willow trees, and if you look closely you may see great blue herons hiding in the weeds and, occasionally, a bald eagle soaring overhead. It's easy to imagine that it must have looked pretty much the same when du Lhut first stepped from his canoe onto the riverbank.

Today, Fond du Lac is a neighborhood of small houses and big gardens. One house, at 13328 West Third Street, blends in well with the other old frame homes nearby. A modest wooden structure with a flat wrap-around porch and steeply pitched roof, it is shaded on three sides by trees, and its shuttered back windows look out over the St. Louis River.

This house, built in 1867 by fur trader Peter J. Peterson, has a significance beyond that of its neighbors—its age. Not only is it the oldest house in the neighborhood, it is also the oldest extant residence in the city.

More than any other of Duluth's neighborhoods, Fond du Lac is a place still dominated by nature—by the St. Louis River, by the massive forests of Jay Cooke State Park, and by the granite bluffs that hold it close to the water. The settled part of Fond du Lac is just a narrow strip of homes lining Highway 23; the rest is still wilderness.

Toward the west, Highway 23 runs right into the vast expanse of Jay Cooke State Park, named for a railroad baron and home to deer, bears, foxes, owls, and hundreds of other animals. Many beautiful, secluded hiking trails here double as cross-country ski trails in the winter. You can even find a pioneer cemetery—just a grassy clearing in the woods with tall, hand-carved tombstones. You have to get close to make out the words, which have been

23 x 8
Fond du Lac and downtown Duluth are a fair distance apart—roughly 14 miles. The city of Duluth is actually shaped like a long thin triangle, narrow at its tips, but eight miles wide at its widest point.

weathered almost smooth over the last hundred years. "Emil Hildor, Infant son of Christian and Petra Wodahl," one reads. "Gone, but not forgotten."

Fond du Lac is still physically isolated from the rest of the city, though it has officially been a part of Duluth since it was annexed in 1895. A two-mile stretch of woods and highway and a small fishing lake separate the last house of Fond du Lac from the first house of the next eastern neighborhood, Gary–New Duluth.

Chippewa or Ojibwa

The Indians of Northern Minnesota called themselves the Anishinabe, the real people. Other Indians called them the Ojibwa, and Europeans modified this to Chippewa. ■ The Ojibwa numbered about fifty thousand at the time of Christopher Columbus's arrival in the New World and lived much farther east than when they were first met by Europeans. Under pressure from the Iroquois, they moved west to the shores of Lake Superior, forcing the Lakota, or Sioux, into the Dakotas.

Take a hike

You can hike either along the river or away from the river and into the hills. The river hike begins in Jay Cooke State Park, which is easy to get to from Fond du Lac. Head west—away from Duluth—and keep to the right. Highway 23 veers to the left, and Highway 210 splits to the right and takes you directly to the park. ■ The park has many hiking trails, most of which begin on the far side of the swinging bridge near the main parking lot. ■ The suspension bridge—which crosses the St. Louis River at a rocky, roiling point—is completely safe, though it squeaks and sways in a way that might delight you or terrify you—or both. Once you're on firm ground again, a whole web of trails takes you deep into the park. You might want to stop at the River Inn by the parking lot for a trail map. In the winter, most of these trails are groomed for cross-country skiing.

The Mission Creek Trail

To hike into the hills, cross the stone bridge on Highway 23 and turn up at 131st Avenue West. Past the playground and the Fond du Lac recreation center is a dirt road blocked by a gate. This road quickly tapers off into a trail—the Mission Creek Trail—that follows the creek through hardwood forest for miles.　■　Parts of the trail are wide and flat, running along the site of long-abandoned railroad beds. At other places, the trail will take you to the tops of gently rolling but fairly high hills. It's an exhilarating feeling to climb one of these hills and to realize that, from the top, you can see no sign at all of civilization—no houses, no power lines, no roads, no other people.

Morgan Park

Anchored by churches at either end, the secluded neighborhood of Morgan Park provides an oasis of quiet in western Duluth. Bordered by the St. Louis River and tucked safely back from noisy Grand Avenue, it's a neighborhood of sturdy, comfortable homes and gently curving, shady streets.

Look closely at those houses—they're concrete, almost all of them. Most of them are painted pretty colors now—green and blue and yellow—but some are still just a weathered gray, the color of concrete. Nearly every house follows the same design: side-by-side, with two front doors, wide porches, and steeply pitched eaves. Nearly every house has a large yard, a back porch, and a parking place in front.

Concrete houses

The sturdy, comfortable homes of Morgan Park recall the company town it once was.

Turn south from Highway 23 onto Commonwealth Avenue. A few minutes drive will take you into the planned community of Morgan Park.

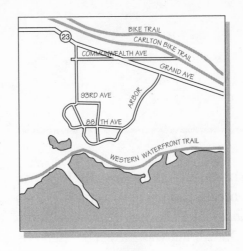

Nearly every house is the same as the one next to it because this neighborhood started out as a company town, a place where everyone had a job at the factory and a roof—a roof identical to the neighbors'—overhead.

Today Morgan Park is a quiet place. But in its heyday, the sound of the whistle blasts from the nearby U.S. Steel plant regularly shook through the neighborhood, calling men to work and announcing shift changes. People set their clocks by the noon whistle, or the six o'clock whistle, and mothers set curfews for their children according to the blasts. Cinders and smoke from the nearby smokestacks drifted over the neighborhood, settling on laundry hanging to dry, on front porches, on the surface of the nearby river. But people didn't mind the pollution much. It represented something to them: the smokestacks belching smoke meant

The benefits of Banner steel fence posts were advertised to farmers throughout the country.

27

jobs—six thousand jobs. And jobs, of course, meant money and security.

In those days, Morgan Park wasn't yet part of Duluth but was a town by itself—a true company town, built and run by U.S. Steel. It was named after J. P. Morgan, the financier who helped organize U.S. Steel back in the 1800s.

U.S. Steel announced plans in 1907 to build the steel plant along the banks of the St. Louis River. From that site, the steel could easily be floated down the river to the Duluth harbor, where it would go out on the big boats to the eastern markets and manufacturing centers. It cost $20 million to build the plant, which made it at the time the largest enterprise in the state.

The Goodfellowship Club

J. P. Morgan reportedly donated the $150,000 needed to build the Goodfellowship Club, which served as the social center of Morgan Park. ■ The club housed a dance floor, gymnasium, swimming pool, auditorium, lecture rooms, and men's and women's reading rooms. ■ It was torn down in 1981 to make way for a smaller, more fuel-efficient building.

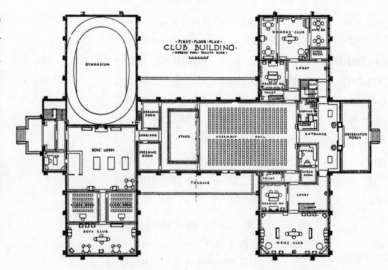

Duluth's population had been growing for years, at the rate of ten thousand people each decade, and the creation of the steel plant was seen as the harbinger of even bigger and better things to come. Duluth, people were sure, would soon rival Pittsburgh in size and influence.

With that population boom, though, housing posed a problem, and U.S. Steel decided to build a "model city" to house its steelworkers. And model it was. The streets were wide and paved. The town included a hospital and a school, and a bunkhouse for bachelors. The huge corporation oversaw every facet of the town's existence—the police force, the water service, the general store, the mail delivery, the school, the community center. The corporation picked up garbage twice a day, and if you neglected to mow your lawn, they'd mow it for you—and charge you a fee.

Morgan Park received a great deal of attention when it was first built back in 1913. Newspapers and magazines across

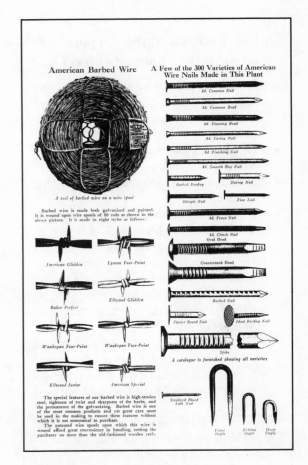

From iron ore, the plant made steel and many finished products.

29

Proud of its contribution in the 1930s to the economy of the region and the nation, U.S. Steel presented these facts and figures in this ad.

the country featured articles about it. At the beginning of World War II, though, U.S. Steel decided it was time to get out of the landlord business. The corporation sold the homes to a realty company, which sold them to the residents. The city of

Ghost factory

The steel plant stands silent now, just a large sand-colored building with broken windows and quiet, empty rooms. Outside, the grass and weeds grow tall. Tarred roads traverse the grounds, some leading nowhere now, others to abandoned gravel pits or pumping stations or to other desolate outbuildings. ■ The chain link fence is locked most of the time, and all residents can see of the once booming U.S. Steel's Duluth Works are the ghostly smokestacks—straight and tall against the sky. And absolutely silent.

Duluth took over the utilities and maintenance. And finally the neighborhood was officially annexed. The company town was a separate town no more.

Though it has been part of Duluth since 1942, Morgan Park is still a self-contained neighborhood. It offers everything you need—grocery stores and a school, laundromats, a ball field, churches and homes. It does not, however, have any bars or liquor stores. And it never did.

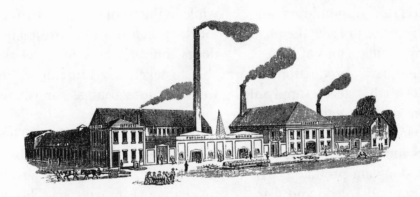

But what would the EPA think?

Two prominent Duluthians thought the area was ripe for more plant capacity than U.S. Steel was building. William Sargent and Jim Bardon, after a "careful computation" wanted "to see the steel plants lining the shores of Lake Superior from Fond du Lac to Two Harbors . . . each striving to outdo its neighbor with smoke and noise."

The steel plant

In its heyday, the steel plant employed more than six thousand people, mostly men from Morgan Park, Gary–New Duluth, and West Duluth. They traipsed off to work every day, carrying lunch buckets and wearing hard hats and work boots, to turn out hundreds of thousands of tons a year of gleaming steel for shipbuilding and automaking. At its peak, in 1950, the plant turned out nearly a million tons of steel.

But shortly after 1950, production began to slacken. Though a steady supply of ore came in from the Iron Range, Duluth was simply too far from the major manufacturing centers and shipping was too expensive to make the plant profitable. The mills in Pittsburgh and Toledo and Gary were modernized, but the Morgan Park plant was left unchanged. The work force dwindled, but the smokestacks continued to belch smoke and cinders until 1970, when the state Pollution Control Agency demanded that something be done. Either clean up, the agency said, or close.

And the plant closed. In November 1971, U.S. Steel laid off thirteen hundred employees. Production continued for a short while in the secondary shops, but it wasn't too long before the entire plant shut its doors forever. Many of its workers were able to take early retirement, but others were left to scrounge for whatever jobs they could find.

There weren't many jobs. The western half of the city had for years been industrial, but by 1970 that had already begun to change. Factories had been closing slowly since the 1950s, and U.S. Steel was one of the last of the big employers to shut down. Interlake Steel, Universal Atlas Cement, the Coolerator plant—one by one, the western Duluth industries and factories had closed over the years, changing the face of western Duluth forever. Take a drive or a bike ride along the St. Louis River and notice the spooky remnants of factories and warehouses that have shut down over the years.

On the other hand, the river is much cleaner than it was. The air is cleaner. And the Western Waterfront Trail, which hugs the river for several miles beginning at Sixty-third Avenue West, follows sparkling blue water alive once again with ducks, herons, and leaping fish.

These giant gears are reminders of the massive machinery that ran the steel plant. They stand near the entrance to the plant at the foot of Eighty-eighth Avenue West.

Riverside

You can get to Riverside many different ways. You can drive, of course, turning your car off Grand Avenue and winding through the steep, narrow neighborhood streets to the river.

Or you might take the bus. Or walk. But you can find other, much more interesting ways to get there.

You can go by boat, for instance—pontoon boat, maybe, or canoe, gliding along the St. Louis River to the pretty little Riverside Marina.

Or you can hike along the Western Waterfront Trail, a crushed limestone path that begins across from the zoo and ends two and a half miles later near the marina. The city built the trail in the 1970s

Perhaps the most beautiful and peaceful way travelers reach Riverside is by canoe.

To reach the marina in Riverside, turn south off Grand Avenue on to Spring Street.

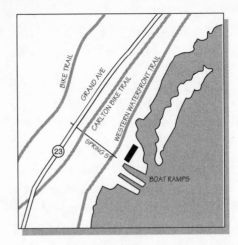

and expanded it in the 1980s, and it winds close to the edge of the St. Louis River.

Or you can bicycle, or in-line skate, or jog along the wide, paved Willard Munger Trail that runs right along the edge of Riverside. This trail is perfectly flat and quite wide, being built on abandoned rail track ground. The trail is planned to eventually run all the way to Minneapolis. It doesn't go quite that far yet, but it does pass through the towns of Finlayson and Moose Lake, on its way to Hinckley, the halfway point. (If you hike the trail in the summer, take time out to hunt for the wild raspberry bushes that grow thick along the riverbank.)

Riverside is a pretty little neighborhood, with houses close together and small, intimate yards, bordered on one side by the Munger Trail and on the other by the St. Louis River.

The marina here was once the site of a booming shipyard. During World War II, the United States Navy operated a shipbuilding facility here, employing hundreds of men. But times change, and, like so

many other industries in the western part of the city, the shipbuilding moved out in the 1950s, leaving Riverside a quieter, sleepier neighborhood.

The industry may be gone, but the people have stayed. No more Navy ships call here, but pleasure boats still dock at the marina—boats with names like "Pair-o-Dice," boats that cruise up and down the St. Louis River on lazy summer days, past the herons and mallards, up the river to Fond du Lac, maybe, and then back home again.

35

Lake Superior Zoological Gardens

With all those great old WPA-era stone buildings and bridges, it's clear that the Duluth Zoo, now called the Lake Superior Zoological Gardens, has been around for a long time. The buildings, both new and old, are scattered across gently rolling wooded acreage in West Duluth, just across the street from the Western Waterfront Trail parking lot.

The main building, constructed in 1931, has two gold lions in front, keeping watch. Inside, cages have been enlarged and modernized in recent years. No longer are the monkeys and chimpanzees crowded into cubicles fronted by prisonlike bars; today,

Although many of the old Zoo buildings have been replaced, the gold lions that guard the entrance remind visitors that the Zoo has been around for a long time.

The Lake Superior Zoo is located at Seventy-second Avenue West and Grand.

the monkeys swing from ropes and tires and leap from branch to branch behind glass.

The zoo really got its start in 1923, when a Duluth printer, Bert Onsgard, rescued a fawn he found wandering through an abandoned logging camp during deer season. He somehow coaxed the frightened animal into his car, brought it home, and then—perhaps an even more amazing feat—coaxed city officials into donating some land for a zoo.

The donated parcel of land lay in Fairmont Park, and the zoo was known as the Fairmont Park Zoo. Within seven years,

Fairmont Park

The zoo is no longer called the Fairmont Park Zoo. Along with the renovations and expansions of the mid-1980s came a fancier name: the Lake Superior Zoological Gardens. But Fairmont Park itself still exists. A large stone pavilion provides the home base for many picnics and reunions, and a whole network of hiking trails snakes through the hills and along the creek bed behind the zoo.

37

Great Moments in Duluth Zoo History

1923   Bert Onsgard returns home with a captured fawn. The start of the Duluth Zoo.

1934   Five hundred thousand visitors stroll through zoo.

1941   Two polar bears battle to the death under the watch of Duluthians.

1950   Fourteen-year-old boy captures a four-hundred-pound horned wild sheep with a flying tackle after the aoudad escaped from the zoo.

1957   Daisy the dog nurses a baby leopard.

1962   Mr. Magoo elicits national outcry.

1963   Mr. Magoo pardoned. First admission charges: twenty-five cents for adults, ten cents for kids.

1965   Visiting nightclub "dancer"—Miss Judy Kelly—donates two boa constrictors and one king snake to zoo.

1969   Big game hunter and wealthy Duluthian Richard L. Griggs donates trophy collection to zoo.

1974   Fewer than 150,000 visitors stroll through zoo.

1976   Prairie dog exhibit opens.

1979   Children's Zoo opens.

1987   State legislature allocates $4 million for expansion.

1989   Wallaby escapes and is killed by passing car.

1990   Second wallaby escapes. It too is killed by a car. Construction hinders visitation. Attendance hovers around 120,000.

1991   Polar shores and Australian Connection exhibits open. Admission: $3.50 for people thirteen and older, $1.50 for kids twelve and younger.

Lake Superior Zoological Gardens

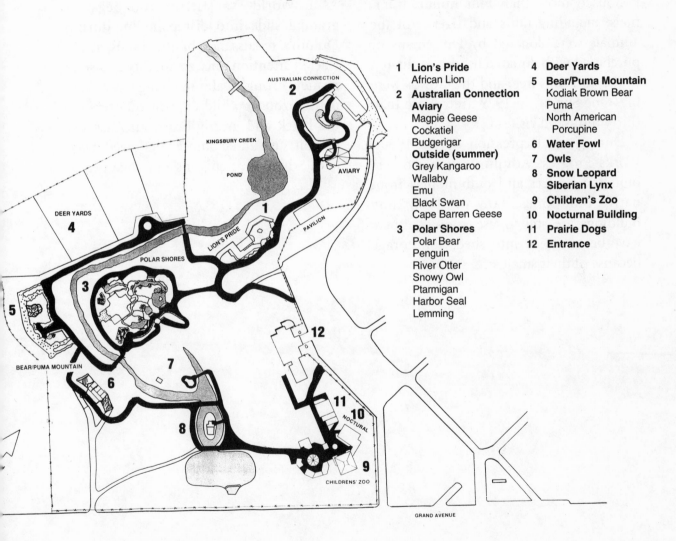

1 **Lion's Pride**
  African Lion

2 **Australian Connection**
  Aviary
  Magpie Geese
  Cockatiel
  Budgerigar
  Outside (summer)
  Grey Kangaroo
  Wallaby
  Emu
  Black Swan
  Cape Barren Geese

3 **Polar Shores**
  Polar Bear
  Penguin
  River Otter
  Snowy Owl
  Ptarmigan
  Harbor Seal
  Lemming

4 **Deer Yards**

5 **Bear/Puma Mountain**
  Kodiak Brown Bear
  Puma
  North American
    Porcupine

6 **Water Fowl**

7 **Owls**

8 **Snow Leopard**
  Siberian Lynx

9 **Children's Zoo**

10 **Nocturnal Building**

11 **Prairie Dogs**

12 **Entrance**

it housed more than four hundred animals, including lions and tigers. All the animals were donated by Duluthians or purchased with donated funds. Admission to the park was free, and the crowds were big. One Sunday in 1929 drew more than thirty thousand visitors.

During the Depression of the 1930s, Works Progress Administration workers built the bridges and outbuildings from native bluestone. Many of these snug buildings are still in use, though others have been turned into sheds for storage because of their small size.

After World War II, the zoo began a gradual slide into disrepair. But during Duluth's renaissance of the 1980s, it attracted attention once again. City and state money brought about changes—a new petting zoo for children, new quarters for the black and grizzly bears, an Australia exhibit, and an elaborate windowed, two-level exhibit for penguins and polar bears.

Mr. Magoo

In 1962, the Duluth Zoo became the site of a national
controversy stemming from the donation of one small, furry
animal—a mongoose. A foreign sailor making a call to
Duluth donated the mongoose to the zoo. Small, cute and
furry, the mongoose attracted an immediate following.
Unfortunately, it also attracted the attention of the United
States Fish and Wildlife Service, which wanted it destroyed.
Mongooses breed quickly and are deadly to many snakes and
bugs, and they are not allowed in the United States.
"Mongoose Given Death Sentence," read a headline in
the *Duluth News-Tribune* of that year.　■ The next day, ten
thousand people showed up at the zoo to get what they
thought might be their last glimpse of the little creature.
Phone calls came into city hall at the rate of one a minute,
demanding that city officials fight the death order.　■ And
they did. News of Mr. Magoo's impending execution spread
across the country, and eventually secretary of the interior
Stewart Udall commuted Mr. Magoo's death sentence.
"There can be no threat of an excess of mongooses being
loosed in Duluth as long as Magoo is not two," Udall said in a
telegram to Duluth officials.　■ Mr. Magoo continued to
bask in the attention; more than 250,000 people visited the
zoo that year to see him. He lived another six years, dining
on his favorite foods of warm tea with sugar, vegetables, and
meat. He died in 1968 of natural causes.

DM&IR Dock No. 6

To see a lively, unusual part of the city, visit Duluth's waterfront. Not the pretty waterfront where the tourists go, Brighton Beach or Canal Park, but the waterfront where the shipyards are, and the wharfs, the part of town where the big ships load and unload their cargo. Down by the ore docks and the grain elevators, where the tourists, and even local residents, seldom venture.

There you'll find workers in Carhartt coveralls guiding bags of pinto beans and

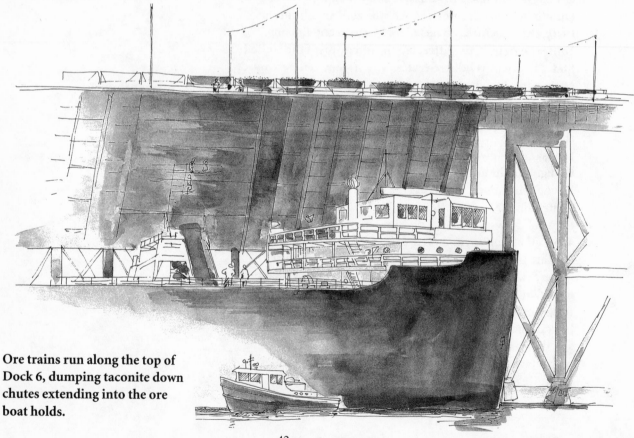

Ore trains run along the top of Dock 6, dumping taconite down chutes extending into the ore boat holds.

42

The docks are located near the Fortieth Avenue West exit off Interstate 35.

mountains of coal into the holds of ships. Red-tailed hawks and snowy owls glide overhead, looking for a wharf rat or a mouse to eat. The dry weeds rustle in the wind that blows, unchecked, off the lake.

In West Duluth you'll find one of the most interesting sites of Duluth's waterfront—the Duluth, Missabe & Iron Range (DM&IR) ore dock No. 6, a mammoth operation built in 1917. From a distance, the dock looks merely large. But the closer you get, the more you realize that it is truly immense.

Dock 6 extends nearly a half mile into St. Louis Bay. Rail cars full of taconite pellets come from all over northern Minnesota to dump their loads here. The dock can hold 150,000 tons of taconite—the weight equivalent of 100,000 automobiles.

The dock's design is a very simple one: it works by gravity. Ore trains run on top of the dock and dump their loads into large hoppers. Chutes from the hoppers are lowered into the holds of the ore ships, and the ore goes rattling down into the hold.

Efficient as it is, though, the dock is

Treasure hunt

If you're curious about the fine points of loading taconite pellets—or you just want to watch the whole thing in operation—you can visit the observation deck located near the DM&IR's dock 6. The observation deck sits near the edge of the DM&IR company parking lot. Getting there is a little tricky. From Interstate 35, take the exit for Fortieth Avenue West. Follow the frontage road about three blocks. It will turn right, then fork. Take the left turn of the fork. You should be able to see the fading and peeling remains of a "Discover Duluth" sign. Follow the winding road into the DM&IR parking lot and the observation area.

43

slowly becoming obsolete. The new thousand-foot ships are too big and too wide to fit underneath the chutes. Seventy-five years ago, Dock 6 dwarfed the cargo ships. Today, some of the vessels are taller than the dock itself.

So the dock has been modified, at the cost of $26 million, by adding conveyor belts to transport the cargo into the bigger ships. But the thousand-footers have created another problem, as well. Because they can hold so much cargo, fewer ships are needed. Fewer dock workers are needed to load the ships. Instead of seven hundred employees, as the DM&IR dock had

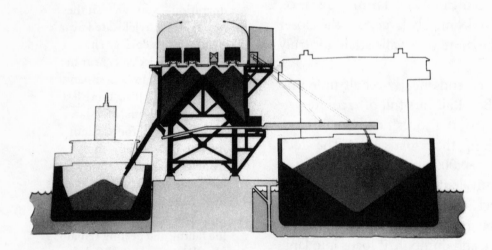

Lake freighters once could be loaded by the gravity feed system shown on the left in this illustration. Now the modern conveyer belt system on the right can transport more than fifty thousand tons of taconite in half a day, evenly distributing the load throughout the ship.

during World War II, dock 6 now employs only about seventy-five people.

Unloading taconite from the railcars is now a year-round activity. Even though ships don't sail between December and April, the Iron Range taconite plants continue to ship the ore to Duluth all winter long. Dock workers unload the taconite into mammoth storage piles nearby. Some Duluthians mark the progress of winter by the growth of the pile; the larger the pile, the closer it must be to spring.

Computers now monitor much of the loading, but the job will never be fully automated. Loading the older chutes still requires a strong arm, and, in the winter, a thick jacket.

The trains of war

"So great was the demand [for iron ore] during the years of World War I that on one day over 200,000 tons were loaded from the Duluth, Missabe and Northern docks alone. This represented 4,700 carloads and meant running ore trains seven miles downhill from the Proctor yard every 15 minutes continuously for 24 hours."

—from *The Minnesota Seaport,* by Ivan Musicant

Oats, peas, beans, and barley grow

The Midwest, America's breadbasket, grows agricultural products for an international marketplace. The oats, peas, beans (more than a half-dozen varieties), and barley are accompanied by wheat, corn, rye, soybeans, sunflower seeds, flax, sugarbeet pellets, onions, and potatoes on boat trips around the world.

■ Although most seeds and grains are shipped in the holds of bulk carriers, others are prepackaged in the Port Authority's bagging facility. The large sacks, stacked on pallets, are easily handled at the other end of their journey.

World port

One would hardly expect to find a world port deep in the center of a continent. The heart of North America, however, is where the grain is grown and the taconite is mined. Fortunately, the Great Lakes and the St. Lawrence Seaway make it possible to ship these products by water, swiftly and economically.

Half of the port's tonnage is taconite produced on Minnesota's Iron Range, most of which is destined for steel mills on the lower Great Lakes.

Other mineral exports include low-sulphur coal from Montana, bentonite, coke, and scrap iron. Some of these products are transferred to other cities in the United States, but many are exported to Europe, Scandinavia and Asia.

Minerals are also imported—European steel for Minnesota metal fabricators, limestone for the taconite, paper-making, sugar beet, and cement industries, and salt to remove ice from our winter roads.

Nonminerals also move through the port—Canadian newsprint and agricultural twine enter; forest and agricultural products leave.

The port is also a transshipment point for heavy equipment and other products, referred to as general cargo. The giant cranes on land as well as the small cranes aboard ships transport this cargo on and off board.

Duluth ships more taconite than any other product, but its towering grain elevators, not ore docks, dominate the port. Since the grain pours down chutes directly into the holds of ships, the elevators stand right at water's edge.

In 1870, Elevator A, the port's first elevator, was built at Michigan Street and Third Avenue East. Sixteen years later it burned to the ground, a common fate for

The harbor view—closeup and panoramic

You will understand the port best if you explore it in two steps. First climb to the top of Enger Tower for a sweeping panoramic view. ■ Then get closeup on a harbor cruise. From the deck of a Vista Fleet boat, you can examine many of the harbor structures as a guide describes them. Sail under the Aerial Lift Bridge and wave to the crews of lakers and ocean-going freighters. ■ Other options for viewing the harbor include the helicopter rides that begin at Bayfront Park and the railroad excursions. Leaving from the Depot, the North Shore Scenic Railroad travels east as far as Two Harbors. The Lake Superior and Mississippi Railroad departs from the Western Waterfront Trail parking lot, traveling west along the St. Louis River.

those wooden structures. It was quickly replaced, however, and within a few years more elevators joined Elevator A on the lake shore.

By the turn of the century, the wooden buildings began to be replaced by the concrete cylinders that now surround the harbor. At any given time, more than 72 million bushels of grain can be held in their bins, ready for shipment around the world.

The last dock

Dock 6 was the sixth ore dock built by the DM&IR Railway. The first four were built of wood and eventually were razed. Dock 5 still stands, to the west of Dock 6, but it was abandoned about a decade ago because of the slackening demand for taconite shipments from Duluth.

Wade Stadium

After more than twenty years, the field of dreams has been restored. Once more the call of peanut vendors mingles with the crack of bats and the cheers of baseball fans. Duluthians are again enjoying hot sunlit afternoons and warm lazy evenings at the ballpark where aspiring young players, hoping for a chance in the majors, and veterans, not willing to hang up their spikes, have come together as the Duluth Dukes.

Wade Stadium was built in 1941 by the Works Progress Administration in a combined effort by the federal government and the city of Duluth. The bricks used in its

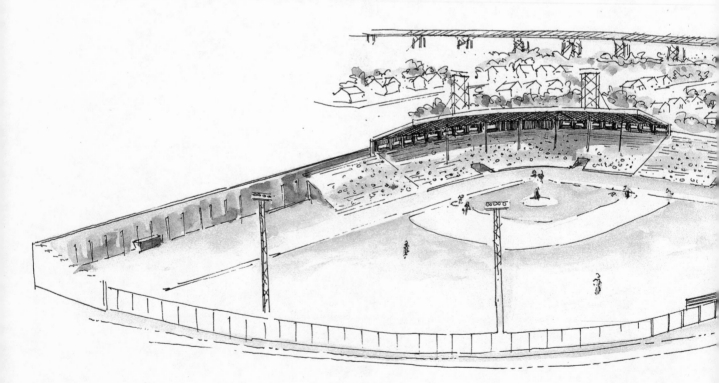

Wade Stadium is located south of Grand at Thirty-fifth Avenue West.

construction had been removed from Grand Avenue during a rebuilding of the street. Many believed the Wade to be one of the finest small stadiums in the country.

Although the Duluth Dukes played their last game on September 8, 1970, the stadium has not been empty during the intervening years. Amateurs continued to use the field, playing more than one hundred

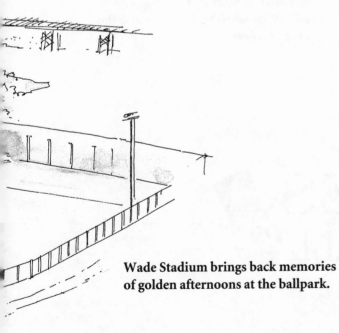

Wade Stadium brings back memories of golden afternoons at the ballpark.

games each year, but watched the facility slowly deteriorate.

In 1984, the Save the Wade organization began raising funds to restore the facility—a new roof for the grandstand, improved lighting, and dugout repairs. Additional seats are needed to accommodate the anticipated crowds, people who are hungry for the sheer pleasure of watching minor league baseball—no huge salaries, no gigantic egos—just people who love to play ball and people who love to watch them do it. Wade Stadium will seat 4,000 of these fans.

Sportscasters beware

Marsh Nelson, Duluth sportscaster, says that the acoustics at Wade Stadium are great. In the press box, you can hear conversations that take place on the field. Unfortunately, the reverse is also true. Marsh narrowly escaped being thrown out of the press box after he scoffed at an umpire's call. What saved him? He was also the official scorer.

Northern League
Roster of Teams

Duluth Dukes

St. Paul Saints

Rochester Aces

Thunder Bay Whiskey Jacks

Sioux City Explorers

Sioux Falls Canaries

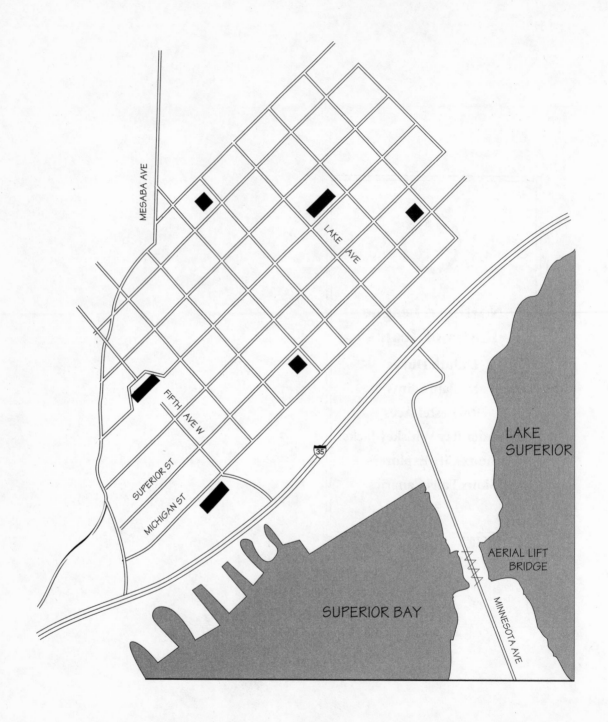

MESABA AVE

LAKE AVE

FIFTH AVE W

SUPERIOR ST

MICHIGAN ST

35

LAKE
SUPERIOR

AERIAL LIFT
BRIDGE

MINNESOTA AVE

SUPERIOR BAY

Downtown

The Downtown once boomed, proudly displaying the tallest office building in the state. A few decades later, people feared that it was dying, with empty storefronts and abandoned buildings.

Today, it thrives again, crisscrossed with skywalks and illuminated with old iron streetlights, crowded with shoppers and walkers and office workers.

One of the most alluring aspects of downtown Duluth is its proximity to the lake. You can see the lake from any avenue and watch the boats from the upper windows of any number of office buildings. In the summertime the gulls head in, as if by clockwork, to wheel above downtowners who choose to eat their lunches outside. And from anywhere downtown, it's just a quick walk to Canal Park and the boardwalk.

This section describes a variety of history-steeped sites: the downtown commercial area; one of the city's first churches; the old Central High School, still one of the focal points of the city; the Civic Center, with its gardens and fountain; and the old Union Depot, now a center for culture and the arts.

But you might want to find other landmarks on your own—some of the shops and restaurants, for instance, or the city's libraries. You can wander through the old Carnegie Library, preserved now as an office building, but just as spectacular as when it first opened a hundred years ago. Or stroll through the modern new library that hugs the western end of downtown and fits into the city's nautical theme, looking, as it does, like an ore boat.

As you walk, drink in the ambiance, the sense of place that defines Duluth: the lake view, the sounds of the foghorn, the busy but friendly pedestrians, the mix of massive old buildings and modern glassed-in shops. A remarkable heart for this city.

Civic Center

On summer afternoons, the air hangs heavy with the spicy fragrance of hundreds of blooming petunias. On winter evenings, the white lights entwined in the bare branches of the flowering crab apple trees sparkle against the snow. Duluth's Civic Center provides more than a place for government business. With its curved, bricked drive, imposing stone

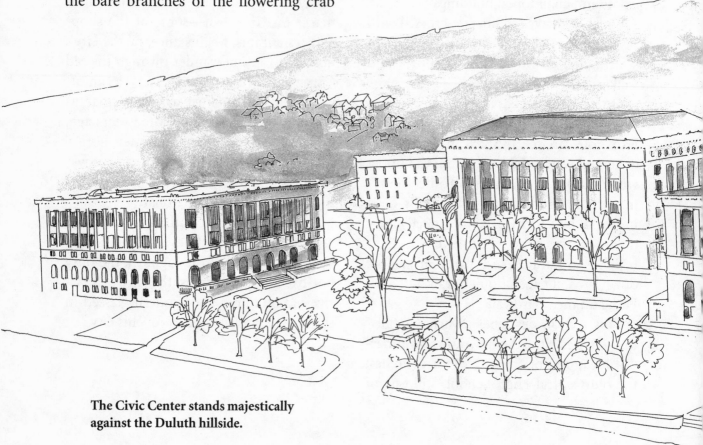

The Civic Center stands majestically against the Duluth hillside.

The Civic Center is located at the west end of downtown Duluth. Drive up the hill from Superior Street at Fifth Avenue West.

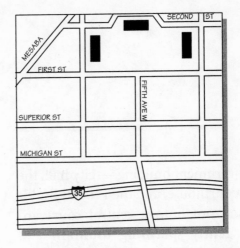

buildings, gardens, and lighted fountain, it graces the city with a showplace of natural and architectural beauty.

The Civic Center sits halfway up Fifth Avenue West, commanding a view of the harbor and the western part of downtown. Appropriately for a city full of parks and trees, the Civic Center is one of the greenest spaces you'll find downtown, with wide green lawns, dozens of flowering crab apple trees, and lush, lavish gardens. The three government buildings—city hall, the county courthouse, and the Federal Building—look out onto a central courtyard with a gently splashing fountain and wooden benches that offer a shady spot to sit and read or have lunch.

Thou shalt not embezzle

A curiosity, if you consider the separation of church and state, is a small stone tablet on the grounds of the Civic Center. It's not readily noticeable, hidden as it is by a bush. See if you can find it. This tablet lists the ten commandments.

Chicago architect Daniel Burnham designed the first of the buildings, the St. Louis County Courthouse, in 1907. Burnham, the father of the "City Beautiful" school of architecture, which favored classical and monumental buildings, selected the site at First Street and Fifth Avenue West because he saw it as the "gateway to the city." This spot at the top of the hill lay just up from what was then a bustling train depot.

The St. Louis County Courthouse is the largest, most ornate, and most imposing of the three Civic Center buildings. It was completed in 1911 at the cost of a million dollars—an incredible sum in those days. Above its front double doors, a frieze proclaims "The people's laws define usages, ordain rights and duties, secure public safety, defend liberty, teach reverence and obedience, and establish justice." Ten stone lion heads keep watch over the yard, perhaps to give weight to those words.

Inside, the building is cool and languid on hot days. The courtrooms are imposingly formal; the winding hallways lead to tucked-away offices and cubbyholes. Keep in mind that these are all public buildings; you don't need an excuse, like a court appearance or a tax payment, to go inside. Feel free to wander the wide, quiet hallways and gaze out from the large upstairs windows to the courtyard below.

Duluth City Hall—the eastern most building—was not built until 1928. Its design was opened to local competition, and architect Thomas Shefchik won the $1,500 prize and the right to design the building. It, too, is imposing, though less ornate than the courthouse—and protected by fewer lions.

Inside the city hall you'll find portrait galleries, of a sort. In the second-floor "hall of mayors" hang portraits of Duluth's former mayors—all men, you'll notice. The first floor walls feature pictures of Duluthians who have devoted years to public service and volunteerism—Duluth's

Beautiful buildings at what seems like bargain prices

1911—St. Louis County Courthouse completed. Total cost: $1 million
1928—Duluth City Hall completed. Total cost: $1 million
1930—Federal building completed. Total cost: $1.2 million

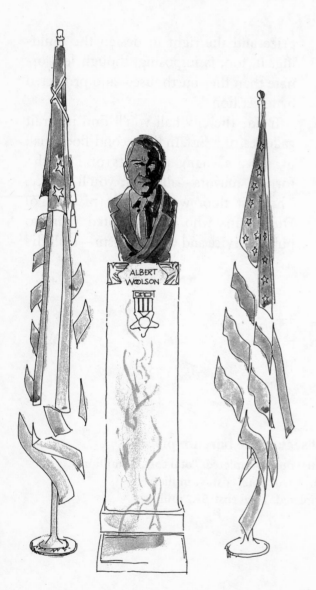

Albert Woolson

In an alcove near the entrance to city hall, a stone bust, a plaque, and an American flag form a memorial to Albert Woolson, the last living soldier who fought in the Union army in the Civil War. ■ On the wall hangs a letter, signed by Woolson when he was 107 years old.

July 12, 1954

To My Fellow Americans,

On April 9, 1865, the terrible war of rebellion ended; the differences between the Union and the Confederacy were forgotten and the North and South were once again united.

As the last survivor of the Union army, I have seen these United States grow into the greatest nation in the history of mankind.

Our sacrifices were not in vain.

Hall of Fame winners. Tucked into alcoves in the same building, monuments commemorate those who fought in the nation's wars.

The city hall's impressive rotunda is often the site of public ceremonies. Every January, for example, the room overflows with people commemorating Martin Luther King Day. And every December, the high ceiling of the rotunda is brushed by the top of a towering Christmas tree decorated with ornaments of construction paper, glue, and glitter, made by the city's schoolchildren.

The Federal Building, built in 1930, was designed by a federal committee and is the plainest and most severe of the three. Its maze of hallways leads to obscure offices and difficult-to-find cubbyholes and labs. At any time of year, the stately calm of the workings of government might be broken by the squeals and laughter of children; a day-care center was established on the ground floor several years ago for the children of downtown employees.

The Civic Center anchors downtown at its western end. From here you can stroll east along First Street's old-fashioned

Bricks that speak

The bricks covering the walkways of the Civic Center are a little different from the bricks that you'll find in other parts of downtown. These bricks carry messages—names, love notes, dates. Among the more intriguing notes: "Thanks Ellie, Love Wally"; one signed "Albert the Cat"; and one that says only "Azuz." ■ The city sold these bricks to help pay for the renovation of downtown. More than a hundred were sold, ensuring that a few Duluthians would be immortalized forever in stone.

bricked streets to bakeries, small shops, and restaurants. Or you can walk down the avenue toward the new ore boat–shaped public library or the famous old Union train depot—now a museum and cultural center, or you can just keep walking all the way across the pedestrian bridge to Bayfront Park, the convention center, and the edge of Lake Superior.

The green, green grass of home
The landscaped grounds of the Civic Center display lush, beautiful flower gardens from May through October. Petunias, flowering crab, and many others all thrive in the fertile soil. So, too, does a less legal plant—marijuana. ■ Over the years, Duluth police have been called in from time to time to uproot the illegal weeds planted by pranksters, who apparently find it amusing to grow this plant in the face of the mayor and the chief of police. ■ As late as 1990, a city employee spotted a three-foot plant in the shadow of city hall.

The Steepest Street

In icy weather, drivers creep up and down Duluth's steep hills, ignoring stop signs and red lights for fear that if they stop, they'll never get started again, or that if they do get started, they'll continue their trip going sideways.

You learn a different sort of driving here. And a different sort of parking. You always turn your wheels when you park on a hill. And you always, always set your parking brake.

For a real adventure, winter or summer, check out the steepest street in town. It's a challenge to get your car up it in anything other than first gear. It's a challenge to bicycle. It's a challenge even to walk it.

Duluth's steepest street has a 26 percent grade

It's Fifth Avenue West, above Fifth Street. On this avenue, drivers of heavily loaded sand trucks no longer even attempt to go up; they have learned to back down, rather than drive up, when conditions are slick. The avenue is so steep the city has installed a handrail so pedestrians can pull themselves up, as a mountain climber might pull on a belay rope.

The street has a 26 percent grade, but the numbers don't do it justice. Get out and walk it. Your legs will be impressed. Once you're at the top and have stopped breathing hard, turn around. Look at what you've accomplished. Your eyes will be impressed, too.

The Incline

Everyone who walks the avenues of Duluth realizes that transportation up the hills must always have been difficult. In 1881 the Highland Improvement Company, a group of wealthy Duluthians who planned to build houses above the downtown business district, solved their future tenants'

The challenge of living in Duluth

When the winter sky clouds over, the plows begin plying Duluth's avenues—or so the legend goes—and it's not too far from the truth. To keep traffic moving, road crews must work throughout a snowstorm. Cities built on the prairie often wait until the storm is over to begin plowing. ■ Student drivers face a real challenge in Duluth, particularly if their cars have manual transmissions. Imagine learning to shift gears when one mistake may bring you crashing into the car behind. ■ Truck drivers are warned to shift into low gear as they descend the hills because the weight of their loads can cause brakes to fail. Each year a few truckers fail to heed the warning and end their journey in the middle of someone's home or business.

transportation problems by contracting with the Duluth Street Railway Company.

Engineer Samuel Diescher designed and constructed the Seventh Avenue West Incline Railway, which ran from Superior Street to the crest of the hill near Eighth Street. On December 2, 1891, the Incline began revenue operations, and many Duluthians gratefully paid the nickel charge to ride the twenty-five-thousand-pound streetcars up and down Seventh Avenue.

Eventually eighty-five miles of street railway tracks served the transportation needs of Duluth's residents. But as the popularity of buses and trolley buses rose in the early 1930s, operation of the Incline Railway decreased, and in 1939 shut down for good.

You will find no evidence of Duluth's once vast street railway system on the streets today, but you can, however, take a ride on a trolley at Depot Square. Although the Depot's trolley is smaller than Duluth's 1910 versions, it is otherwise similar, and the quarter-mile round trip from Depot Square Station to the end of the museum, past the storefronts and businesses located on Railroad Street, provides an excellent way to experience travel in Duluth's boomtown past.

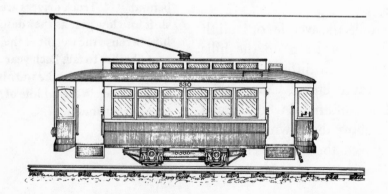

The Depot

The train depot in downtown Duluth bustles these days, crowded with people coming and going, wandering the hallways, staring wide-eyed at the trains, hurrying to climb aboard.

It's just like in the old days, except for one thing: these days, the trains don't move.

Built in 1892, the lovely, turreted brick building sits at the foot of Fifth Avenue West, anchoring downtown. For decades,

**The Depot is
an excellent example of the
Chateauesque style of architecture**

The Depot sits at Fifth Avenue West and Michigan Street, just one block south of Duluth's main street and three blocks off Interstate 35.

the Depot was a major point of entry to Duluth, the largest terminal for all the railroads.

But over the years, travel changed. Passenger train traffic decreased. More people bought automobiles. Greyhound expanded its franchise into Duluth. The airport came through. For a long while, the depot was closed, locked and shuttered against the cold Minnesota winters.

But though it was abandoned, it wasn't forgotten. For years, residents knew that they wanted the solid old building to be preserved. In the 1970s, it opened up again as a cultural center. It is now called the St. Louis County Heritage & Arts Center—though still known, affectionately, as "The Depot"—and it houses an art gallery, three museums, and offices for various cultural organizations, such as the Duluth Ballet, the Duluth-Superior Symphony Orchestra, and the Duluth Playhouse.

When you walk in the front door, you're immediately struck by the diversity of activities. To your right is a small theater, where the Duluth Playhouse and the ballet

Take a close look

Flanked by substantial, yet graceful, towers, the Depot with its beautiful curving roof line is one of the country's best examples of Chateauesque architecture. ■ Midwestern materials were used in its construction: brick from Chaska, Minnesota, sandstone from Hinkley, the brownstone trim from Portage, Wisconsin, limestone from Bedford, Indiana, granite from Ortonville, Minnesota, and slate for the roof from Pennsylvania.

69

perform. Straight ahead, a small art gallery features local artists. And to the left the Depot opens up into a whole series of rooms—a gift shop, a balcony gallery, big glass display cases in the Great Hall, a handful of offices, and other museums.

The trains

People from across the country have made special trips to Duluth to see the vintage trains in the Lake Superior Museum of Transportation, which is housed on the lowest level of the Depot.

Visitors can view engines ranging from the tiny Minnetonka, just twenty-seven and a half feet long to the mighty Mallet, five times its length. Along with the engines, a variety of other railroad cars and equipment will give you a picture of railroad transportation across many decades.

Walking through one of the passenger cars, you might imagine that you were a lumber baron dining in luxury and sleeping in comfort. Children, however, will

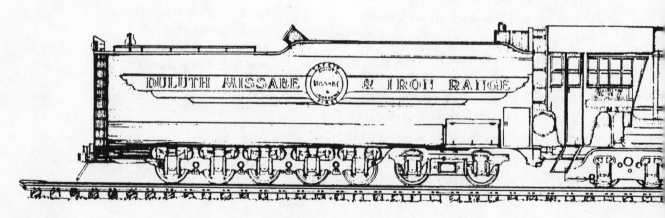

Minuscule to massive

The Minnetonka, built in 1870, looks like a toy train next to the mighty Mallet. It's hard to believe that with its woodburning engine it pulled heavy loads of rails and ties.

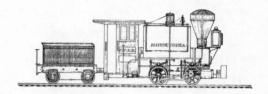

One of only a few locomotives remaining from the Civil War era, the William Crooks, built in 1861 for the St. Paul and Pacific Railroad, was the first locomotive in Minnesota.

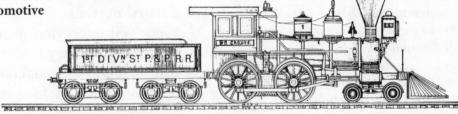

The Mallet, one of the largest and most powerful steam locomotives ever constructed, pulled trains of almost two hundred cars of iron ore from the Mesabi and Vermilion Ranges to the ore docks.

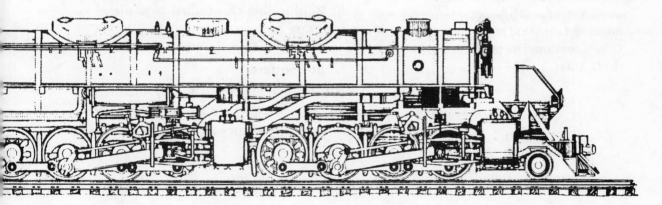

The immigrants

Only the very brave could consider the journey to be an adventure. Most immigrants must have been terrified by the trip and by their unfamiliar destination—the long ocean journey by boat, probably in steerage; arrival at Ellis Island without a word of English; the two-day train trip to Minnesota. ■ One can imagine the joy felt by the immigrants who were reunited with relatives in this very room. For thousands of others, however, the Depot's Immigration Room was just one more stop on their search for a better life. ■ Many immigrants found jobs in the iron mines and forests of Minnesota. Others continued on to homestead in the Dakotas.

pretend that they are engineers on the Mallet. When the wheels slowly begin to turn and the whistle blows, you may expect the train shed doors to open and the Mallet to begin another journey to the Iron Range.

Excursion train

When you finish your imaginary ride on the Mallet, you may want to experience a real train ride. Throughout the summer months you can head over to the North Shore Scenic Railroad, located in the west end of the Depot, and take an hour-and-a-half train ride to Lester River or a day-long round trip excursion up the North Shore to Two Harbors. The tours are narrated by experienced guides. You will ride in comfortable cars pulled by a diesel locomotive or in the self-propelled Budd Car.

Depot Square

For a much shorter trip, hop on the Depot trolley and ride along the streets of turn-of-the-century Duluth. Depot Square, its streets lined with businesses and shops, historically accurate replicas of actual buildings, recreates life when the Union Depot was at its busiest, fifty trains arriving and departing each day. The shop window displays, ranging from hardware to haberdashery, suggest that Duluth was a prosperous city.

Sieur DuLhut Room

Step farther back in time when you visit the St. Louis County Historical Society's Sieur DuLhut Room, which features exhibits of Indians, voyageurs, explorers, and fur traders—as well as a replica of a fur trading post. The Society also displays logging tools and a model logging camp in the Logging and Lumbering Room and 1910 household furnishings in a parlor and kitchen.

Habitat Tree

Created especially for children, the A. M. Chisholm Museum's Habitat Tree is a two-story walk-through wildlife exhibit. Children and adults explore the exhibit by climbing through the inside of the giant, hollow tree. Look for seasonal and topical exhibits regularly presented by the Chisholm Museum, one of the nation's first children's museums.

Performing arts

The Depot is the cultural center of Duluth. Alongside its three museums, the Depot houses five arts organizations: the Duluth Art Institute, The Duluth Ballet, Matinee Musicale, The Duluth Playhouse, and Duluth-Superior Symphony Orchestra.

Some of these groups present exhibits, others perform on a regular schedule, most offer classes for both children and adults.

The balcony and entrance galleries usually contain art exhibits curated by the Duluth Art Institute. In their lower level studios, artists conduct workshops in painting, ceramics and fiber art.

Each season the Duluth-Superior Symphony Orchestra, founded more than sixty years ago, performs seven classical concerts and three pop concerts at the Duluth Entertainment and Convention Center.

Matinee Musicale, founded in 1900, brings to Duluth famous international performers as well as gifted young musicians just at the start of their careers.

Dance came to Duluth much later as The Duluth Ballet was not formed until 1965. It's repertoire now includes classical, modern, and jazz works. Thousands of Duluthians have been introduced to the joys of dance through its classes.

Playfront

Children will shop or look at museum exhibits for only so many hours—then they're ready for action. ■ Just a few blocks from downtown Duluth, and a short walk from the Depot, the adventure playground at Playfront Park will entrance any child. Sturdy wooden beams provide climbing equipment for the body, and ships and castles for the imagination. ■ Cross Interstate 35 on Fifth Avenue West, turning right into the park. If you are on foot, you can walk across the Fifth Avenue West overpass or walk the skywalk to the DECC, though this would be a long hike for a three-year-old.

The Duluth Playhouse, one the oldest community theaters in the United States, presents an eight-play season in the Depot Theater. Dramas, comedies, musicals, and a children's play are presented each year.

The Depot is a clearinghouse for information about these and other arts organizations in Duluth.

Bayfront Park

Built at water's edge, the stage at Bayfront Park, protected by a huge yellow sail, is the location for many summer events including the famous Bayfront Blues Festival. It is also home to community gatherings such as the Fourthfest and the Duluth International Folk Festival and a variety of other performances. ■ Strolling along the boardwalk towards Canal Park, you will pass the Duluth Entertainment and Convention Center and cross the Minnesota Slip on a footbridge behind the William A. Irvin ore boat.

Alworth Building

No one in recent years has come to Duluth to stare at the skyline. While downtown has plenty of attractive buildings, refurbished storefronts, and charming new streetlights, Duluth simply doesn't have an awe-inspiring view of towering skyscrapers like you find in New York, Chicago, or even Minneapolis.

But back in 1910, the gawkers certainly turned out. That was the year the tallest office building in Minnesota was completed—the

The Alworth Building stands in the center of downtown Duluth, at the corner of Second Avenue West and Superior Street.

Alworth Building, right on Second Avenue West and Superior Street in downtown Duluth.

All sixteen stories of it.

A 16-STORY MODERN REINFORCED STEEL STRUCTURE, THAT DWARFS THE TOWER OF BABEL TO A COTTAGE, screamed a headline in the *Duluth News-Tribune* of the day.

The steel-framed, brick-covered office tower of the Alworth Building was designed by Daniel Burnham, the same architect who designed Duluth's Civic Center. Commissioned by Marshall Alworth, who had made his fortune in real estate and iron ore, the Alworth Building was a marvel, containing some 275 offices on its sixteen floors.

Not long after, of course, Minneapolis and St. Paul began erecting much higher buildings, and the Alworth Building no longer caused stiff necks and wide eyes. Nobody pays it much attention anymore, now that the World Trade Center and the IDS building are just a few hours away.

But eighty years after its doors first opened, the Alworth Building has been unmatched locally. It is still the tallest building in Duluth.

Look up

Many interesting boomtown landmarks hide behind modern downtown storefronts. As you walk down Superior Street, look up to see fascinating architectural details that are not usually noticed by pedestrians.

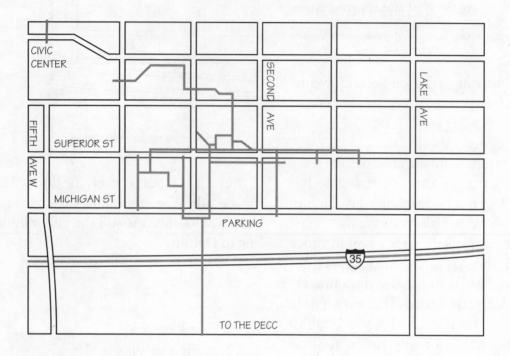

The Skywalks

More than two miles of enclosed skywalks, which keep you out of the weather, link Duluth's downtown buildings. Beginning at city hall on Fourth Avenue West and snaking and zipping and twisting through downtown, the skywalks cross First Street and Superior Street and head east all the way to First Avenue East. One long wing branches out and takes pedestrians all the way to the Duluth Entertainment and Convention Center (DECC), down by the lake front. ■ In the winter, it's a great way to get around downtown without having to worry about muddying your shoes, climbing over snowbanks, or wearing your heavy coat. ■ In all seasons, you'll find determined-looking people striding past, arms swinging, feet clad in tennis shoes, ears covered by headphones. The skywalk system has become a popular walking route for downtown office workers, senior citizens, recovering heart patients, and others who are interested in their health but who don't care to venture outside.

Duluth from Superior

When you're in Duluth, you can only see parts of the city. But from Superior you can see the broad expanse of Duluth stretched out along the bay—all of downtown, the waterfront, and the eastern side of town, and most of the western half. The view from Superior truly captures a sense of the city clinging precariously to the face of a cliff, which appears from that vantage point to be almost vertical.　■　It is difficult and costly to build on Duluth's steep bedrock hillside. Water lines must be buried deep to protect them from winter cold. Streets must be carved into solid rock. A few decades ago, before almost every family owned an automobile, more homes perched high above Piedmont Avenue. They could be reached only by steep wooden staircases.　■　The city now owns many parcels of land along Skyline Parkway, protecting the view for future generations.

Sacred Heart Cathedral

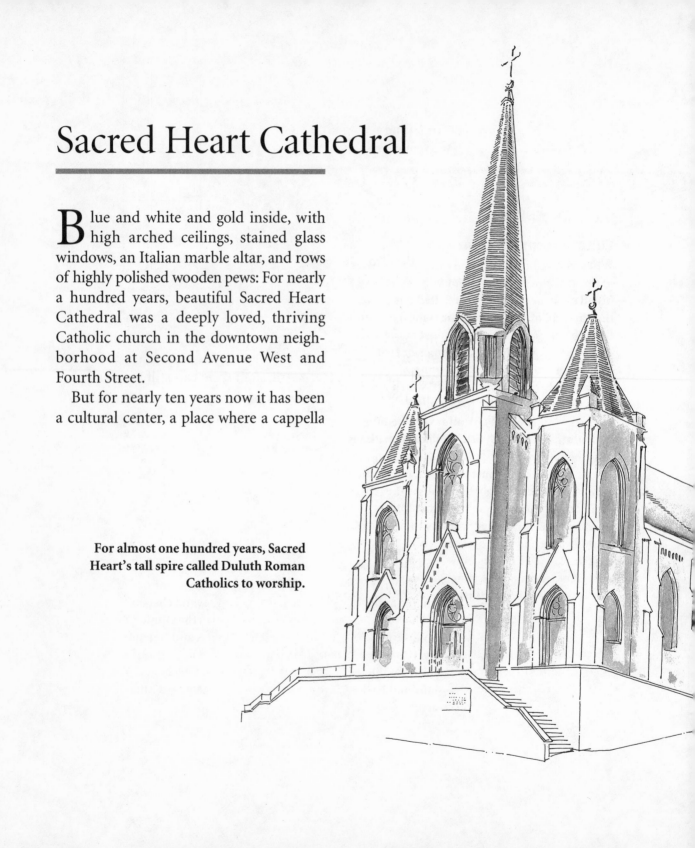

Blue and white and gold inside, with high arched ceilings, stained glass windows, an Italian marble altar, and rows of highly polished wooden pews: For nearly a hundred years, beautiful Sacred Heart Cathedral was a deeply loved, thriving Catholic church in the downtown neighborhood at Second Avenue West and Fourth Street.

But for nearly ten years now it has been a cultural center, a place where a cappella

For almost one hundred years, Sacred Heart's tall spire called Duluth Roman Catholics to worship.

Sacred Heart is located on Fourth
Street between Second and
Third Avenue West.

5TH STREET

SACRED HEART

4TH STREET

3RD STREET

3RD AVE W · 2ND AVE W · 1ST AVE W · LAKE AVE

2ND STREET

1ST STREET

choirs sing at Christmas and people gather for concerts. Its name now is John Chebul-Sacred Heart, combining the cathedral's name with that of the priest who began the parish back in the late 1800s.

Sacred Heart's cornerstone was laid in the summer of 1894; the formal dedication came two years later. This cathedral was built to replace the original Sacred Heart Church, which burned in 1892. It lasted nearly a hundred years, closing as a church in 1985, when the parish merged with the parish of St. Mary Star of the Sea.

But parishioners and neighbors would not let it die. They began a fund and raised money to preserve the building. The cathedral's tall spire can still be seen from blocks around, a testament to the skills of its builders and the enduring loyalty of its admirers.

A city of churches

Duluth is a city of churches and synagogues. Immigrants brought their religious faith along on their journey to America and soon after their arrival built houses of worship. Nearly fifty religious organizations now have one or more buildings in Duluth, the architecture ranging from simple wood chapels to stone cathedrals. ■ The multitude of denominations reflects the ethnic heritage of Duluth's people—Roman Catholics from Italy, France, and Ireland; Lutherans from Germany, Norway, Denmark, Sweden, and Finland; Methodists and Anglicans from England; Eastern Orthodox from Greece and Serbia; Jews from Germany and Eastern Europe; Presbyterians from Scotland; and many others, of course.

Across the street stands another large brick building, which served as the cathedral school for many years. The building is no longer a school, but it remains a place of good works and goodwill. As the Damiano Center, it houses a clothing exchange and soup kitchen for the poor, a counseling office for battered women and battering men, and an agency that helps the homeless find places to stay.

Many churches welcome your visit, so step inside during the day and view the sunlight streaming through beautiful stained glass windows.

Central High School

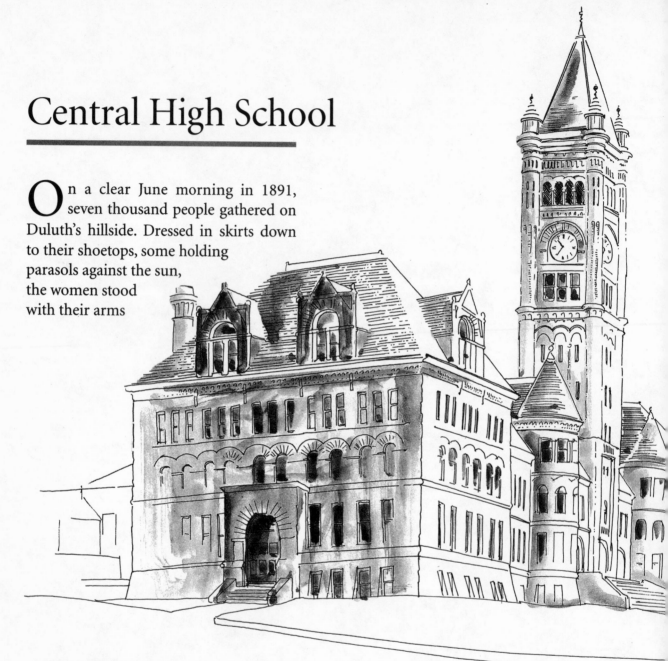

On a clear June morning in 1891, seven thousand people gathered on Duluth's hillside. Dressed in skirts down to their shoetops, some holding parasols against the sun, the women stood with their arms

Central High School's imposing presence must have impressed young people with the importance of education.

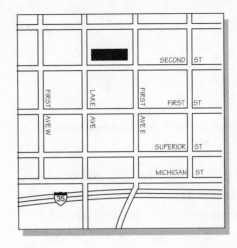

Central High School stands high above Second Street between Lake Avenue and First Avenue East.

---

protectively around the shoulders of their children. All this fuss, after all, was really for them—the children, the future of Duluth.

In workboots and mustaches and string ties, the men gathered near the front, where the speeches were being made. All had come to watch the cornerstone being laid for a new school, an impressive four-story redstone building with a clock tower that would be visible for miles. Young Duluth was undertaking an ambitious project, and the crowd knew that when it was completed, the school was sure to be the most imposing building in town.

Speeches by school superintendent Robert Denfeld and populist firebrand Ignatius Donnelly stirred the crowd to pride and excitement. Denfeld told them that upon completion of the new school,

"at the head of the lakes shall stand the proudest city in the Northwest!"

And Donnelly, well-known for his inspiring, flowery speeches, proclaimed, "We have come to rear a temple not to superstition or cruelty, but to intellect, a temple

Kids and crowds

As Central was being built, Duluth's student population soared. In the five years leading up to 1891, Duluth's student body increased from 1,600 to more than 5,000. By 1920, more than 17,000 students attended Duluth's public schools.

85

which shall last for hundreds of years and in which the greatest of all things—the human mind—should be developed!"

The crowd cheered with enthusiasm.

Duluth was still a rowdy boomtown in those days, a town of saloons and shipyards and muddy streets. But the citizens looked ahead to the future, to a time when Duluth would be more civilized, more genteel—to the days when it would truly become the Zenith city civic leaders anticipated it would be.

It had been only thirty-five years since the city's first schoolhouse had been built. That modest one-room wooden building had served the town well, but rapidly growing Duluth needed a larger, more modern space to educate its children. This new building was to be impressive, splendid, the talk of the Midwest.

Duluthians paid $500,000 for the Central High School building, which had a gymnasium, chandeliers, oak woodwork, and large, airy classrooms. Stone gargoyles and cherubs stared out over outer doorways and windows.

Central officially opened in 1892, with the United States secretary of the interior presiding over the ceremonies. Newspapers hailed it as "the most complete high school in America." Its name, of course, came

A leader in education

Duluth set the standards in Minnesota education before the turn of the century. Just two years before Central High School was built, Duluth became the first city in the state to provide free textbooks for students.

from its location; the building is perched halfway up Lake Avenue, the steep street that divides eastern Duluth from western.

More than a hundred years later, the building still stands, still magnificent, still splendid, still a landmark. Its 230-foot-high clock tower still looms over the central part of the city; its stone gargoyles still glower over downtown.

But Central is a school no longer.

For seventy-nine years, high school students climbed its worn steps daily from September through June. Now it holds the offices of the school district's administrative staff.

Before New York had subways

A tradition of officially sanctioned graffiti flourished at Central. In the spring, seniors were allowed to climb the school's clock tower for their one and only authorized view from the top. They were also allowed to write on the inside walls of the tower on their way up.

No equity like inequity

Pay equity in Duluth in 1920: Women teachers averaged $120 a month. Male teachers averaged $171 a month.

Central closed as a school in 1971, after long years of hard use had begun to take their toll. In the 1960s, the handcrafted woodwork and open stairways came to be seen as fire hazards; modern codes called for enclosed stairways and less flammable building materials. The suspended balcony in the school's auditorium began to experience a decided bounce, which gave an extra thrill to enthusiastic pep rallies. Finally, one night, chunks of plaster fell from the cafeteria ceiling, crashing to the floor and crushing tables and chairs below.

Clearly, something had to be done. The school, still magnificent and imposing on the outside, had become dangerous to its students inside. So the school board voted to build the new Central High—a disk-shaped, ultramodern building a couple of miles away on top of the hill.

Plans called for Old Central to be torn down. But locals couldn't bear to demolish the beautiful old building. Historians

A look around

The Central Administration Building, once in the dynamic heart of the city, now sits in a neighborhood that has seen better days. The houses around it have been carved up into rental apartments; Second Street, which faces the building's front door, has become a wide, fast thoroughfare for motorists heading to East Duluth. You won't find too many landmarks east or west of the school—homes, a scattering of businesses, a few parking lots. ■ But if you head down steep Lake Avenue, in just two blocks you'll be on Superior Street, Duluth's main street. From here, you can climb the stairs that lead to the interesting and unique Freeway Park, a blooming, tree-studded, surprisingly quiet park built atop Interstate 35. The park runs for about six blocks and has wide sidewalks, wooden benches, and an bronze sculpture from Duluth's Russian sister city of Petrozavodsk. From the park, pedestrians can either walk down to the Lakewalk, which runs to Canal Park, or east to the Fitger's-on-the-Lake historic district. ■ Just remember—it's a steep walk back up the hill to Central, if that's where you left your car.

and preservationists fought the idea and finally saved Central as a historic landmark. After extensive remodeling—including a new copper roof—the building reopened in 1975 as the headquarters of the school district's administration.

Some objected, of course, complaining that if the building was safe for administration it would also be safe for students. New Central, they argued, had been a waste of money. But others countered that while the refurbished building could handle the lighter load of office work, it could not take the pounding that thousands of high school students would give it.

And really, both sides had won: the students had their new school with the old name, and the impressive temple of learning remains to loom over downtown for another hundred years.

Hotel Duluth

In its day, it was the grand hotel of the city. Built in the mid-1920s by a Milwaukee firm, the Hotel Duluth was massive, ornate, and very much in vogue. Located at the eastern corner of downtown on Third Avenue East and Superior Street, the fourteen-story building attracted hundreds of prestigious guests, including President John F. Kennedy.

Hotel Duluth, at the corner of Second Avenue East and Superior Street, anchors the eastern end of downtown.

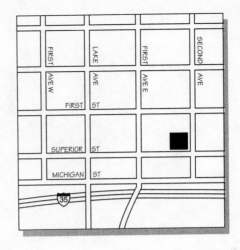

In addition to its four hundred guest rooms, the hotel had stylish party rooms—the small, opulent Moorish Room, the Italian Renaissance-style lobby, the large, exquisite ballroom—where meetings and New Year's parties and celebrations took place.

For years, it was the most prestigious place to stay in town. But in the 1960s and 70s, new hotels were built; and the grand old hotel, which had neither swimming pool nor electronic arcade, could no longer compete. The hotel closed, and in 1981 it was turned into apartments and renamed the Greysolon Plaza.

Since nothing else anywhere in Duluth can match the gold leaf and tile and marble of the ballroom and the Moorish Room, the building has never lost its popularity. These rooms are all still popular places for high school reunions, wedding receptions, and private parties. In 1993, several scenes in the Hollywood movie *Iron Will* were filmed in the hotel's Moorish Room and lobby.

For years the bar in the old Hotel Duluth was known as the Black Bear Lounge, in honor of a 350-pound black bear that wandered into the hotel in the fall of 1929. In an exciting front-page newspaper story in the *Duluth News-Tribune,* a nameless reporter breathlessly tells how the bear followed a pickup truck carrying a load of fish from the East End to downtown, where the truck went one way—up the hill, and the bear went another—into the hotel. ■ The bear apparently tried to break into the hotel coffee shop—presumably looking for food—but the night watchman kept him at bay by throwing chairs at him until a brave Sergeant LeBeau of the Duluth Police Department arrived on the scene and felled the bear with a single rifle shot to the head. ■ The bear's carcass is now on display at Grandma's Saloon & Deli in Canal Park, a famous eatery and repository of Duluth memorabilia.

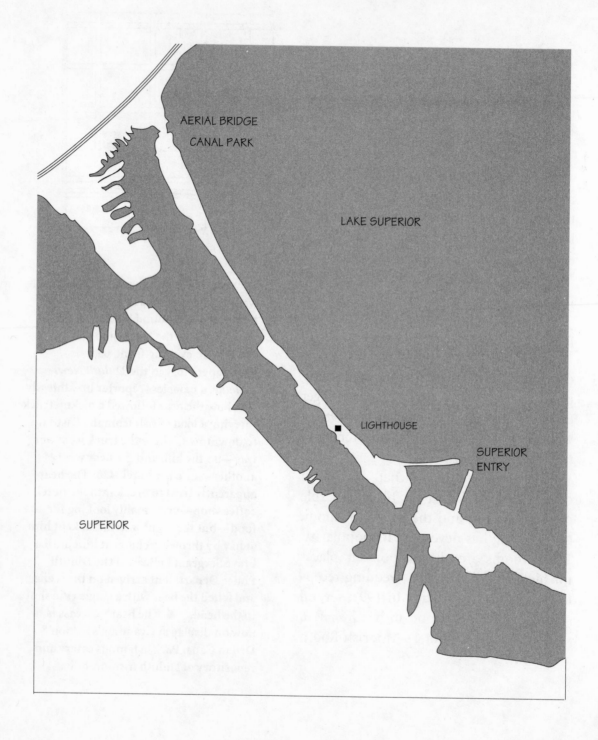

Waterfront

More than anything else, Lake Superior defines Duluth. The lake provides the water highway to the east coast and the Atlantic Ocean; the lake sends heavy fog over the town for days at a time in the summer; the lake ensures that the city will be blanketed in snow all winter.

Duluth's waterfront has many personalities. At Canal Park, you will find a tourist center, a pretty little area with shops and seagulls and doughnut stands and street musicians.

Here you can climb on the boulders that edge the lake and skip rocks across the water. Here you can watch the lakers and the ocean vessels gliding under the Aerial Lift Bridge any day during most of the year. East from Canal Park you can wander the Lakewalk, a European style promenade, built on the old rail grade, that attracts both locals and visitors for strolls late into the evening.

Further west, the waterfront is all business. Tall grain elevators and rattling coal docks are home to snowy owls and red-shouldered hawks, who glide over the rusty railroad tracks, searching for rats and mice. Big, oceangoing ships take on their loads of taconite or pinto beans or powdered milk.

Along Park Point, you get another feel for the waterfront. On the bay side, protected from the wind, watch families of mallards paddling close to shore. Members of the Duluth Rowing Club practice their strokes in the calm bay. Stand on the lake side, your face into the wind, and feel the power of the unchecked weather. In the winter, walk the frozen beach, climbing over splinters of blue-green ice, scattered like shards of glass at water's edge.

At the end of the Point a hiking trail leads to the crumbling remains of an old brick lighthouse, a reminder of the old days when the town was just beginning.

Stroll the waterfront. Get to know the city's different personalities. Become friendly with the lake.

Aerial Lift Bridge

Quick, what's the first thing you think about when you think about Duluth—besides Lake Superior? For most people it is Duluth's most famous landmark, the Aerial Lift Bridge. That old steel-beamed bridge has drawn millions of tourists to the waterfront over the years, to crane their necks as they watch its deck slowly ascend 120 feet. The rising deck moves out of the way to make room for stately oceangoing ships, for one of the

Duluth's best-known landmark is not a building but a bridge.

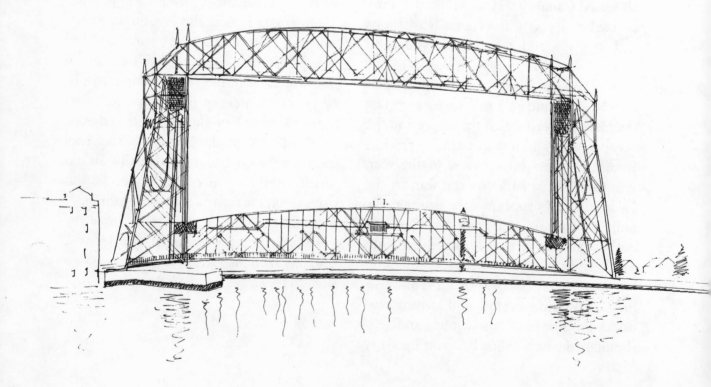

You can see the Aerial Bridge from most parts of the city. To get there, take the Lake Avenue exit off Interstate 35 or turn south on Lake Avenue from Superior Street.

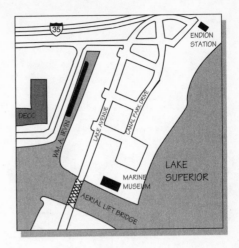

fleet of tourist boats, or for skittery, gliding catamarans, in an always entertaining, always slightly amazing spectacle.

The bridge wasn't constructed to be a tourist attraction, of course. It was built in 1905 for purely practical reasons: to span the channel that separates downtown Duluth from Park Point, and to allow the massive lakers and oceangoing vessels into the harbor.

Until 1871, Park Point had been connected to the rest of Duluth. But that year engineers began digging the canal that would open up the harbor to shipping traffic. It was great for the shipping industry, but it turned the Point into an island.

For the next thirty years, people got over to the Point however they could. In the winter, they gingerly crossed on the ice. In the summer, they took one of the frequent ten-cent ferries. A rope walkway spanned the canal briefly before the turn of the century. It was there only during months when there was no shipping, and it was wobbly and unpredictable enough that people sometimes resorted to crawling across it.

Clearly, the area needed a bridge. It had to be high enough to allow masted vessels through, and small enough to be affordable. Duluth's city engineers searched for a suitable design and finally found one in France, where the Seine River passes through the city of Rouen.

As first designed, Duluth's bridge didn't rise—it was suspended from a track. The original bridge had a gondola, which hung from cables and held up to six automobiles. Cars and pedestrians boarded at one side and the trolley slowly traveled across the channel to the other side. An adventurous trip each time, no doubt.

During its first year, the bridge reportedly transported thirty-three thousand people to and from Park Point on one summer day. But as Duluth grew and more people could afford cars, the strain on the shuttle increased; and in 1930 the bridge

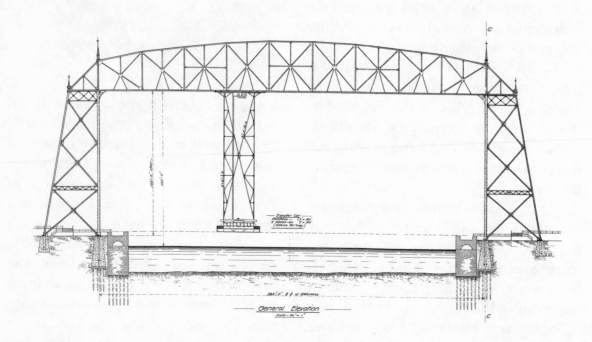

General Elevation
Scale - 20' = 1'

DESIGN FOR
SUSPENDED CAR TRANSFER
OVER
SHIP CANAL, DULUTH, MINN.
SUBMITTED BY
The Gillette-Herzog Mfg. Co.
Minneapolis, Minn.

C.A.P. Turner — Engineer.

Feb. 1901   Patent Applied for   Design #3394

96

was remodeled. The side towers were raised and reinforced, the trolley platform was removed, and engineers installed in its place a rising road deck. That 1930s-refurbished model is the same bridge that stands at the lakefront today—a maze of steel beams and girders like an Erector set, with a small window-lined house perched above, where the bridge operators work.

Visitors to Canal Park have plenty of warning before the bridge rises. All you have to do is listen. First, you'll hear the sonorous monotone blast of the ship, signaling the bridge operator to raise the deck. The flat, mournful call comes as one long blast, then a short, then a long, then a short.

If you have young children along, this is your signal to put their hands (or yours) over their ears. Things will soon get very noisy, and unprepared children can be terrified by the racket.

Within moments, the bridge responds—a higher, shorter blast. Then the bells begin—a shrill vibrating jangle that warns motorists and pedestrians that they have only a few moments to get off the bridge. Barricades, like those at railroad crossings, come down, and lights flash. It's all quite a spectacle.

It's fascinating to stand on the pier directly underneath the bridge and watch as the deck goes up. You can see the beams beneath, somehow comforting in their size and girth. You can see the massive cables, as thick as a person's waist, or thicker. And you can see the 970-ton counterweights as they offset the weight of the rising and descending deck.

That's a good vantage point, too, for watching the ships pass. They glide almost noiselessly under the bridge, the sides of

The bridge operator watches this dial as the bridge slowly rises.

The Endion Depot

The stone and brick visitors' center along the Canal Park Lakewalk wasn't always a visitors center. And it wasn't always at Canal Park. ■ The structure was built as a train depot in 1899. Made of sandstone hewn from the Kettle River quarry just south of town, it was constructed at the foot of Fifteenth Avenue East, below London Road, in what was known as the Endion neighborhood. ■ The depot provided the first "suburban" stop along the lakeshore. ■ When the depot shut down, the building was named to the National Register of Historic Places. In the mid-1980s, the city began to renovate its waterfront and plan for a freeway to pass by where the depot stood. ■ The building would be lost, city officials said, if it was left between the freeway and the inaccessible lakeshore. So it was moved. Early on a spring morning, workers loaded it onto a flatbed truck and slowly hauled it two miles to a grassy area near Canal Park, where it now stands. The trip took all day.

the big new thousand-footers perilously close to the walls of the narrow canal. The stirred-up water slaps at the sides of the boat and the edges of the pier. Sailors sometimes stand and wave at the throngs of locals and tourists who gather at water's edge to watch.

And then the bells begin again, and the bridge deck slowly descends.

The Aerial Bridge is built almost entirely of Iron Range steel and has been painted various sober colors over the years. It has been forest green, it has been black, it has been midnight blue.

Today, it is a silver-white, and when it is illuminated at night with spotlights,

the whole structure turns into a glowing focal point of Duluth's refurbished waterfront.

Canal Park

The park at the foot of Lake Avenue, that small green space that stretches along the lake near the Aerial Bridge, has long been a popular spot with locals. In recent years, after a multimillion-dollar facelift, it has

become popular with tourists, as well.

Here you can stand at water's edge and watch the big boats sail past; you can feed the pushy, mouthy gulls that have grown bold from an indulgent diet of tourists' french fries; you can stroll the boardwalk and watch the waves burst like fireworks on the rocks and change color with the sky.

Here, too, you can buy cotton candy and hamburgers and tacky souvenirs made of seashells and plastic. Or you can buy an expensive, fragrant cup of cappuccino or a hand-painted Lake Superior T-shirt or an entire Gore-Tex rainsuit.

And you can spend hours people watching—taking in the in-line skaters, or the dog-walkers, or the sidewalk musicians, or the blonde, tanned sun-worshippers lying in the grass. Canal Park has become, in recent years, a summerlong lakeshore festival.

At one time, the area was a seedy hangout where sailors gathered to drink at the old Sand Bar and spend their afterhours in Joe Huie's Cafe. To get to the bridge you had to thread your way past factories, a junkyard, and any number of warehouses.

But gradually the area began to change. The old Sand Bar, enlarged and remodeled, reopened under the name Grandma's Saloon & Deli, now one of the city's most popular nightspots. In the 1980s, the city of Duluth began transforming the rest of Canal Park into a picturesque tourist mecca.

Now a wooden boardwalk runs from Canal Park eastward along the shore all the way to Leif Erikson Park, two miles away. Vendors hawk hot dogs and doughnuts and souvenirs. Musicians strum their guitars or play their saxophones along the rocky shore.

The factories and warehouses have been renovated into upscale shops, but with a Northland twist. They sell quality outdoor gear, wild rice, and hand-appliqued loon sweatshirts.

With its park benches, swinging wooden

signs, and bricked streets and sidewalks, Canal Park may not look anything like a real waterfront area. The sailors and long-shoremen, it's true, don't spend much time there anymore. They have been replaced by tourists who throng the lakeshore, eager to watch the wheeling, screeching gulls, feel the spray of the lake, and gaze with awe and admiration as the mammoth ore boats glide past.

Duluth Ship Canal

There are stories, and then there is the truth. Some sources tell a wonderful story of how Duluth came to build its ship canal. But unfortunately, only part of it is true. Here's the story.

Once upon a time, just after the Civil War, the people of Duluth decided they wanted a passageway between Lake Superior and the natural harbor formed by the

102

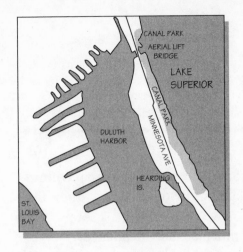

sand-covered spit of land known as Minnesota Point.

They had tried to find other harbors. In the late 1860s they built a breakwater out into Lake Superior, manufacturing a harbor off the Point. The town's wiser residents knew that such a manufactured harbor would never be able to weather the lake's severe storms. And they were right. The only way to get a harbor, they said, was to cut a canal through the Point, allowing passageway into the protected bay.

So in the fall of 1870, the town decided to do just that. A steam shovel crew began digging a canal through the sand and rock of Minnesota Point.

This made the people in the neighboring town of Superior angry. Superior was competing with Duluth at that time to become the transportation mecca of the upper Great Lakes. Duluth already had the edge, because Duluth had a railroad and Superior did not. Superior wanted the shipping industry for itself.

So Superior's city officials enlisted the help of the state of Wisconsin and the

Piloting a ship through the narrow Duluth canal is tricky business. Winds and crosscurrents only make it more difficult. And it doesn't really make much difference which way the wind is blowing. Lake captains say that a stiff wind from the northwest causes the most problems in getting through the canal, but a northeast wind is more troublesome once they're in the harbor. ■ Because the canal is so narrow, captains usually line up the bow of the ship with the entry to the canal from a point at least two miles out.

United States government to stop Duluth's canal digging. In other words, they filed suit.

That much actually happened.

Here the legend begins. According to it, a Kansas judge heard arguments against Duluth's digging the canal. He agreed with the residents of Superior and issued an injunction to halt the digging. His ruling came on a Friday, and Duluthians received the news by telegram. But the mayor had a plan. The federal marshal who was to deliver the injunction in person wouldn't get to Duluth until Monday. That gave the city the weekend to act.

Word went out, and thousands of Duluthians turned out with pickaxes and shovels. They began to dig. They worked in shifts, round the clock, morning, noon

Big ships

Iron ore—now in the form of taconite pellets—makes up the bulk of the cargo shipped out of Duluth. A century ago, the largest vessels on the lakes carried about three thousand tons. Now the largest carriers stretch to one thousand feet long and can hold up to sixty thousand tons.

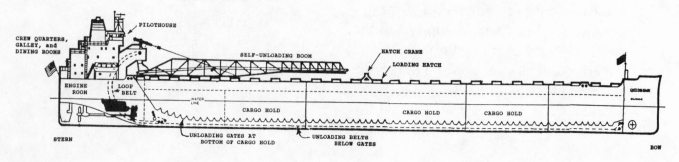

CREW QUARTERS, GALLEY, and DINING ROOMS

PILOTHOUSE

SELF-UNLOADING BOOM

HATCH CRANE

LOADING HATCH

ENGINE ROOM

LOOP BELT

WATER LINE

CARGO HOLD

CARGO HOLD

CARGO HOLD

STERN

UNLOADING GATES AT BOTTOM OF CARGO HOLD

UNLOADING BELTS BELOW GATES

BOW

104

and night, from Friday night until Monday morning. The men toiled, the women brought food and coffee and the children hauled away what rocks and debris they could handle. Prostitutes worked next to churchmen, lumberjacks next to bankers.

By late Sunday, a tiny rivulet trickled through the ditch, and by Monday morning a strong current of spring runoff gushed through the canal. As the federal marshal stepped off the train, injunction in hand, the waters burst through. A small tugboat sailed through the new canal, blowing its horn merrily in celebration and triumph. The tired and dirty crowd cheered. And the mayor told the marshal that he was free to stop the water, if he could.

It's a great legend. But it's not true.

Here's what really happened, according to reports in the *Duluth Minnesotian*, a newspaper of the time.

Superior did, indeed, file suit to stop the canal, but the courts moved slowly and

Parking a thousand-footer

People who have trouble parallel parking wish that they could pull up next to a parking space and slide sideways into it. Side thrusters on freighters make it possible for something like that to happen.

■ "Salties," the oceangoing ships must be towed into the harbor by tugboats, but the Great Lakes freighters enter the harbor and navigate into narrow slips under their own power. Only their side-thrusting engines (and the great skill of the captains and crews) make this feat possible.

nothing had been decided by late fall of 1870. Work on the canal halted when winter set in, and resumed early in the spring of 1871. When the excavation workers hit frozen ground, some citizens did come forward to help with shovels, picks, and two kegs of gunpowder. But nothing nearly so dramatic happened as the entire town working side-by-side against the clock.

Superior did, indeed, win the injunction to stop the canal, but the ruling came on June 12, more than a month after the canal was already completed.

The canal soon proved profitable to both cities; by World War I the harbor was loading more cargo than any other harbor in the world. In 1913, nearly twelve thousand ships entered the Duluth-Superior harbor to haul away Iron Range ore and other goods.

Today, traffic in the harbor has decreased considerably, though the volume of cargo has remained about the same. Bigger, more efficient ships can haul much heavier loads than ships of fifty years ago. Now, about thirteen hundred vessels visit the port of Duluth-Superior each season.

The Duluth-Superior harbor is the largest port on the Great Lakes, but it no longer ranks in the top ten among all United States ports.

Marine Museum

As you stand behind the ship's wheel in the Marine Museum's pilot house and gaze out over Lake Superior, it takes very little imagination to place yourself high above the water in an oceangoing ship. Charts are laid out on the table behind you. Your navigation aids are ready. The romance and adventure of the sea capture you as you pass through the ship canal, beginning a journey around the world.

The turn-of-the-century pilot house is

just one of the attractions that bring almost half a million visitors (as many as six thousand a day) to the Canal Park Visitors Center and Marine Museum, which is run by the U.S. Army Corps of Engineers. The exhibits include full-size cabin replicas, furnished with artifacts salvaged from ships.

You can learn about the geology, history, and economy of the port through audio-visual presentations as well as through the exhibits. Lake Superior's great depth is shown by a large relief map. Beautifully crafted model ships demonstrate how ship building has changed during the past three hundred years. A huge engine suggests the power of ships that ply the Great Lakes. Well-designed displays interpret the area's major industries.

Telescopes located on the upper level allow you to get a closeup view of ships,

Queen of the Lakes

For a taste of life on the high seas, step aboard the William A. Irvin, the six-hundred-foot freighter that was once the flagship of United States Steel's Great Lakes fleet. You can tour the working portions of the ship, the pilot house and engine room, as well as the beautifully restored staterooms. Guides, including former sailors, provide information and tell tales of life on the lakes. ■ The Irvin, a floating boomtown landmark, is docked in the Minnesota Slip between Canal Park and the Duluth Entertainment and Convention Center.

and the Museum's free *Great Lakes Shipping Guide* with its four-color illustrations of flags and smokestack markings will help you identify the ships you see.

The entire museum is a wonderful introduction to the Great Lakes and the port.

The Corps of Engineers has other more practical tasks in the Duluth harbor and throughout the St. Lawrence Seaway. They keep navigation open throughout this great inland waterway of lakes and canals, maintaining locks and harbors, and dredging channels.

You can't stop progress

Duluth is in a constant race against the progress made by ship builders. As ships are made larger to carry ever increasing cargo loads, deeper and wider channels must be carved if Duluth is to remain competitive with other ports. The floating dredges you see in the harbor clear these deep trenches to at least twenty-seven feet, the depth of the St. Lawrence Seaway, expanding them when necessary and also removing the silt carried into the harbor by the St. Louis River. ■ Captains who stray from the marked channels will find their ships deeply mired in the harbor mud. Only the hardy little tugs will be able to pull them free.

Minnesota Point Lighthouse

At the end of a mile and a half trail through tall red pines, in an open area surrounded by grass and water and sky, stands an old brick lighthouse.

It's actually only the shell of a lighthouse now—lensless, roofless, a broken cylinder of red Ohio brick reaching for the sky.

But for about twenty years in the late 1800s, this lighthouse at the end of Minnesota Point, a seven-mile-long finger of sand that divides Lake Superior from the

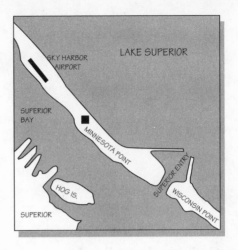

St. Louis River, was the most important structure around. When it was completed in 1859, the lighthouse stood fifty feet high and guarded the very edge of the river's mouth. Its French-made lenses—the finest available—cast their beams through the thickest fog, warning ships of the rocky shoreline.

The first lighthouse keeper, R. H. Barrett, lived with his wife and family on the end of the desolate Point. Their job was to maintain the lenses and operate the foghorn, which sounded to let ships know how close they were to shore.

In those days, the foghorn was a simple affair; it consisted of a tin horn and a strong pair of lungs. During foggy weather—which can last for days in this part of the country—Barrett and his wife

Minnesota Point

Its official name is Minnesota Point, but everybody calls it Park Point. Flat and straight, the point is only wide enough for one street, which runs five miles from the foot of the Aerial Lift Bridge to the Sky Harbor Airport. In the summer, bicyclists, in-line skaters, and runners, as well as hundreds of cars, throng the street. The annual rummage sale and the annual art fair ensure that the neighborhood is particularly crowded for two weekends each summer. ■ Houses line both sides of the street, of course—old summer cabins that have been refurbished and elaborate brand-new mansions—and almost every house has a lake or bay view. ■ In the area's early days, Indians lived on Park Point in the summer, moving inland in the winter when the winds and snow lashed across the Point. The Ojibwa lost the Point in the Treaty of 1854, and the area became a haven of summer cabins for the white people who lived in Duluth.

Visit the beach

Sunbathers and squealing children leaping over waves crowd the white sand beach of Park Point in the busy summer. But few people venture past the beach house, volleyball net, and lifeguard station. Those who do, however, can trudge along the beach—their feet sinking, the sand pushing up between their toes—for another two miles.

took turns spending hours blowing into the tin horn. Nearby settlers dubbed the mournful-sounding foghorn "Barrett's Cow."

The lighthouse was in use only until 1878. By then, the ever-shifting river outlet had moved east more than a quarter of a mile. Concrete piers were built to stabilize the river mouth, and a new lighthouse was built about a half mile from the original. The highly prized French lenses were transferred to the new beacon, where they remained until 1963.

The original lighthouse fell into disrepair. Strong winds and weather took their toll, until the structure now stands only thirty-five feet high and is crumbling at the top. Still, it remains an important landmark. For years it served as "point zero" for all surveys of the region; along its base you can still see the brass mark that indicates that exact point.

Take a hike

The hike to the lighthouse begins at the Sky Harbor Airport just past the recreation area parking lot. You have two ways to go—through the woods or along the beach. Whichever way you choose, you'll have to get past the barred gates of the airport. Don't be frightened off by the "no trespassing" signs; the land to the left of the airport driveway is public property and leads to the wooded trail.　■　It's about a mile and a half walk through the tall, swaying trees, along a path cushioned with sand and pine needles. In the winter, the trail is straight and smooth enough to ski or snowshoe. It will take you past a service road and old cabin foundations—Park Point once held a number of summer cottages—and boat landings on the bay side. The lighthouse isn't quite at the end of the Point. Once you get there, you may want to keep walking to the concrete piers—a good place to sit, have a picnic lunch, and watch the gulls and sandpipers and other water birds dip and soar.

In 1975, the lighthouse was named to the National Register of Historic Places, though nothing has been done to restore or maintain it. Scrawled over on the inside with graffiti from countless high school sweethearts and overgrown outside with tansy and beach grass, the lighthouse now keeps watch only over sand dunes and birds' nests and groves of scraggly, wind-blown trees.

Birding the Point

Park Point is probably the best place in the city to bird-watch. Behind the Bayside Market, along Hearding Island, you'll find a terrific area to spot a variety of gulls, terns, and shorebirds. ■ At the end of the Point, down near the recreation area, hundreds of warblers come through every spring during the yearly migration. A foggy May day is the best time for spotting them; the warblers won't fly under those conditions, and the leaves are still small enough then so that you can get a clear view of the birds on the nearly bare branches. ■ Farther down the Point, between the Sky Harbor Airport and the old lighthouse, serious birders can really do some heavy birding. Shorebirds and sandpipers roam up and down the beach, and inland you can see just about anything. Keep your eyes open for the old great horned owl that has lived in these woods for twenty years.

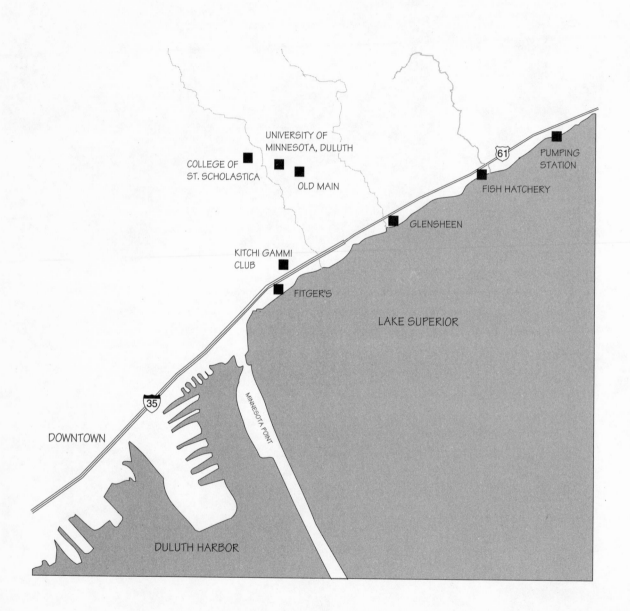

Eastern Duluth

If you like to walk, consider a stroll through East Duluth. The eastern half of the city welcomes you with a blend of wide, shady residential streets, historic East End homes, and large expanses of ravines and parklands.

But there's much more to the eastern half of the city than that. Head up into the Woodland neighborhood, for instance, and explore Hartley Field, a vast six-hundred-acre park crisscrossed with hiking and cross-country ski trails. Here, on hot summer days, the smell of clover is strong and the tall grass tickles your legs. Or walk past the oddly shaped house at 2102 Woodland Avenue—now a private home, but in the late 1800s the Glen Avon streetcar station.

Or stop some Sunday morning at one of the East End's massive old churches— Our Lady of the Holy Rosary Cathedral, at the corner of Fourth Street and Wallace Avenue (at approximately Twenty-seventh Avenue East); St. Paul's Episcopal, at Seventeenth Avenue East and Superior Street; Pilgrim Congregational, on Twenty-third Avenue East and Fourth Street; or Glen Avon Presbyterian, up in Woodland. Built in the early years of this century, all provide fine examples of stone and brick work and stained glass.

Also in the East End you'll find the colleges, such as the old Normal School campus, its most spectacular building recently destroyed by fire, but its other old buildings still standing proudly. Or the University of Minnesota, Duluth campus, a sprawling, modern conglomeration of classrooms, libraries, and offices. Or the beautiful campus of the College of St. Scholastica, set back in the woods and looking almost like it grew there, built of native stone and wood.

It's a comfortable collection of neighborhoods, the city's eastern half. A neighborhood for walking. A neighborhood for gawking. A neighborhood for exploring.

Fitger's

The low-slung brick building with the smokestack and the spectacular lake view sits on the corner of Superior Street and Seventh Avenue East. Today it houses a luxury hotel, a couple of restaurants, and a smattering of boutiques. A new parking ramp provides spaces for plenty of cars. A patio behind the building gives visitors a place to sit and watch the boats go by.

But Fitger's hasn't always been an upscale shopping center. At one time, it was filled with a couple of hundred burly workers and several large copper vats.

The brewery that rose to fame as Fitger's

Fitger's stands on the lake side of Superior Street at Seventh Avenue East.

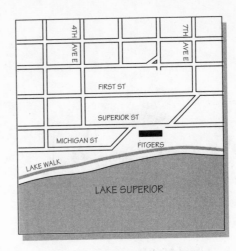

first opened in 1859, when Duluth had only a couple of hundred settlers. It employed only four people and was often on the verge of closing. The business struggled by for a dozen years, barely making ends meet. By 1870, times had improved, the

Fitger's, now a luxury hotel and up-scale shopping center, was once a brewery.

At the Races

Every Wednesday evening all summer long, the Duluth Keel Boat Club holds sailboat races out on the lake. The best view in town is from the park bench next to Fitger's—or, if you prefer some kind of refreshment while you're watching, the umbrella tables at Sir Benedict's Tavern. There you can watch the dozens of sailboats—some with plain white sails, others with colorful spinnakers—dip and tack and glide on the glassy surface of the lake.

Solid pioneer character

Alfred Merritt wrote of settlers during the Panic of 1857: "I want to speak of the general honesty of the pioneers of the Northwest by telling you what Captain Ben Sweet, of the steamer "North Star" said of them when times were so hard, and no one had money. The captain took down over seven hundred passengers and took their notes in payment for their transportation. Of these, all paid their notes with one exception . . . When one considers that these seven hundred people scattered all over the New England States, and then in every case, with that one exception, paid their notes, it is a remarkable testimonial to the rugged honesty of the early pioneer."

population had grown, and the brewery was solidly on its feet, producing about five thousand barrels of beer a year.

About this time August Fitger arrived in town. Fitger had learned the art of brewing back in his homeland of Germany, and his dream was to own a brewery of his own in America. By 1884, his dream had been realized. He bought the Duluth brewery, expanded the operation, and began using his own recipe. The beer brewed there has been known as Fitger's ever since.

August Fitger modernized and streamlined the brewery, and by World War I it was one of the largest and most up-to-date in Minnesota. Then came Prohibition. Rather than shut down entirely, the brewing company survived by switching to root beer, candy, and "near beer."

Good times returned with the end of Prohibition, and in its heyday, Fitger's employed 250 people and turned out more than 150,000 barrels of beer a year.

After World War II it became difficult for small, local breweries to survive. Popular though Fitger's was, it didn't stand a chance against the cheaper prices and intensive advertising of the large national competitors. The growing popularity of big breweries such as Anheuser Busch and Miller caused hundreds of small local breweries to close all over the country. Fitger's shut its doors in 1972, and for years the building sat abandoned, a chain link fence keeping out the curious, the smokestack silent, the copper vats empty.

With the renovation of the brewery and the opening of the shopping mall, though, a Wisconsin brewery bought the rights to the Fitger's name. And even though it's no longer Duluth-brewed, once again visitors can pull up a stool in just about any local bar and pop open the top of a cold Fitger's beer.

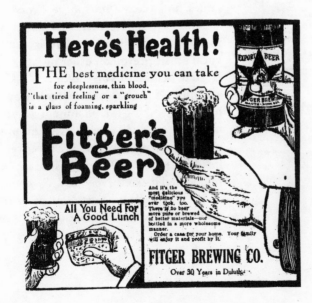

This Fitger's Beer ad suggested that a one-beer lunch was both nutritious and delicious.

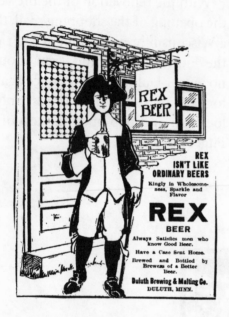

Many believe it is Lake Superior water that gave Duluth beers their mellow flavor.

British Tavern

Across the street from Fitger's and next door to the Kitchi Gammi Club sits a small British pub. It flies the British flag outside, and a small swinging wooden sign announces its name: Sir Benedict's Tavern-on-the-Lake. Outside the bright blue building, umbrella tables and chairs offer a comfortable seat and an unobstructed view of the lake. Inside, you'll find dozens of different ales and stouts, small wooden tables, and a cozy atmosphere. Every Wednesday night local musicians gather to play bluegrass together; live jazz and vocal music prevail on other nights. Hard to believe this all was once a gas station. ■ But it was. Sir Ben's, now a popular drinking establishment, was for many years a Shell station, with gas pumps outside and mechanics in greasy coveralls inside. A local family purchased it in 1977, remodeled it extensively, added a cooler, dozens of small wooden tables, and some photographs of Great Britain.

Kitchi Gammi Club

People think of it as a small piece of England in Duluth, this imposing building with the leaded glass windows, high ceilings, and Tudor trim. The Kitchi Gammi Club has been a refuge for the wealthy and influential since it was incorporated in 1883.

For years, women weren't allowed to enter through the front door but were dropped off at the side entrance. And until the mid-1980s women who entered the club did so as spouses, daughters, or guests of members. Not as members.

The Kitchi Gammi Club, at Ninth Avenue East and Superior Street is a short walk from Fitger's.

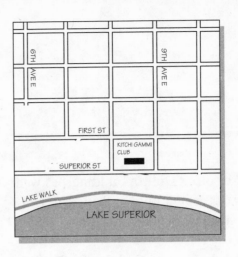

The Kitchi Gammi Club was the first private men's club in the state. It has been in its current location at Ninth Avenue East and Superior Street since 1913, in a building designed by New York architect Bertram Goodhue. Goodhue designed a

With its leaded glass windows, the Kitchi Gammi Club looks like a Tudor country house.

Duluth is one of the smallest cities in the country to have such a lavish private club. A 1990 article in *Fortune* magazine listed the Kitchi Gammi Club alongside New York City's Knickerbocker Club and Boston's Somerset Club. The Kitch, according to *Fortune,* "attracts all the local corporate brass and then some. Betty Ford, passing through Duluth, took home a jar of Kitchi Gammi Club Horseradish to hubby, she fancied the stuff so."

125

handful of other Duluth buildings, as well as many of the buildings at Princeton University and Wellesley and Bryn Mawr colleges.

The Kitchi Gammi Club has an English Gothic design, with leaded glass windows, cherry wood, and oak. The floors creak underfoot. Coats and ties are required of the men at all times, except in the basement pub. Outside, in the summer, servers bring guests cool drinks on the wide stone porch, under the shady trees.

The first members of the club were shipbuilders and mine owners; at least eighty-three ships on the Great Lakes carried the names of club members.

The club grounds are surrounded by a wrought-iron fence and look out on Lake Superior. Though the extension of Interstate 35 zips past right in front of the club's front doors, chances are no one notices it

This somber looking carving of an Indian keeps watch outside the Kitchi Gammi Club.

126

much; the freeway runs underground at this point, ensuring that the view of the lake and the Wednesday evening sailing races aren't impaired.

Directly across the street from the Kitchi Gammi Club is another Bertram Goodhue building, the Hartley Building. The similarities between the two buildings are quite pronounced: both are of brick, with leaded glass windows. The Hartley Building, though, is much smaller.

Old Main

Tucked down a narrow, quiet side street of eastern Duluth, between a grove of trees and a rocky ravine, stands a group of massive old buildings. These magnificent structures, nearly one hundred years old, were once the site of learning and laughing, a place where students gathered to study and stroll the rolling green lawns. Quiet now, with no more students, two of the buildings are empty, their windows boarded over.

The arches, all that remain of Old Main, are at Twenty-third Avenue East and Fifth Street.

The four brick buildings, with their tile roofs and arched doorways, were built in 1898 as a women's college for training teachers. The college, known as the Duluth Normal School, opened in 1902 with a class of ninety-one students and ten instructors. The requirements were minimal—a student needed at least an eighth-grade education to be admitted. And tuition was free for anyone who promised to teach at least two years at a public school within the state.

The campus, at Twenty-third Avenue East and Fifth Street, has always been in a quiet neighborhood. One high-water mark for excitement in the school's early days

Publisher's note

In the winter of 1993 Old Main was destroyed by fire. Only the arches that framed the doors remain, although a city park will be developed on the grounds. ■ Because the college was important to so many area residents, we chose to leave this chapter in the book.

129

came when a wandering herd of cows spread out over the lawn and munched its grass.

The Normal School grew quietly and steadily and in 1921 became the Duluth State Teachers College—a coed institution. Just a few years later, in 1939, the enrollment had swelled to seven hundred students.

Over time, the University of Minnesota system absorbed the teachers college, and it became the headquarters for the Duluth branch. A few years later, university officials purchased a large piece of land about a mile away for the site of the new campus, which is still in use.

But the old Normal School remains. Its solid buildings have been used as extra classrooms for UMD, as office space for the state agricultural extension service, as a university theater, and as dormitories.

Big Campus

UMD today occupies more than sixty buildings. The main campus, less than a mile from the Normal School campus, is bordered by College Street and St. Marie Street, just off of Woodland Avenue. UMD also oversees the Natural Resources Research Institute on the edge of town, Glensheen Mansion, and the limnological lab by the Lester River.

Education is big business in Duluth. UMD employs more than 500 academics and 900 civil servants. St. Scholastica employs more than 150 faculty members, with a total work force of 350.

St. Scholastica

If you're cruising up College Street to visit the UMD campus, you might spot, just up the road, two gray stone towers. Those are the anchors for Tower Hall, the main building of the College of St. Scholastica. ■ Mother Scholastica Kerst purchased a parcel of wooded land in the wilds of Duluth and opened her girls' school in 1908. The campus now contains two main classroom buildings, dormitories, a priory, and a nursing home, all nestled on 160 acres of woods. The woods are crisscrossed with hiking trails and rimmed by a rocky little creek. ■ Tower Hall, with its slate steps and quiet, dim hallways, still has the hushed feeling of a convent—unless students are around, when it becomes as noisy and boisterous as any campus. ■ Behind Tower Hall, flower and vegetable gardens are still tended by the Benedictine sisters who live there. Gethsemane Cemetery, where many of the nuns are buried, lies just past the soccer field. And the wooded trails beyond cut through the pine, birch, and aspen forest, home to deer and fox and owls and the occasional bear.

Glensheen

If the western half of Duluth has always been the industrial, working-class heart of the city, the eastern half has been the domain of the rich and influential. Here lived, in the city's early days, mining barons and lumber kings, shipbuilders and high-powered attorneys, in exquisite homes they built along the rocky shore of Lake Superior.

Spaced along London Road and climbing the steep eastern hillsides, stately mansions date from the late 1800s and early

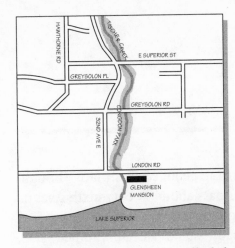

Glensheen, located at Thirty-third Avenue East and London Road, is almost hidden behind stately trees.

1900s. With their turrets and stained glass windows, their carriage houses and rolling green lawns, these homes offer magnificent examples of interesting and innovative architecture. Duluth's old East End houses are among the most beautiful in the country, and since many of them are clustered in the same neighborhoods rather than scattered across town, they are easy to find. If you are interested in architecture, you'll want to spend an afternoon looking at these places.

If you travel by car, start at Sixteenth Avenue East and cruise slowly along Fourth Street. Swivel your head; beautiful old homes stand on both sides of the tree-lined street. When you get to Twenty-Sixth Avenue East, come back along Third Street. Then head east again along Second Street, and come back along First. Those four streets will give you a good glimpse of the varied architecture of the East End homes.

Many of the houses closer to downtown were carved up into apartments and rental property years ago, and some show signs of hard wear. Under the influence of a

nonprofit citizens group called the Duluth Preservation Alliance, others have been renovated in recent years. Several have been turned into elegant bed-and-breakfasts, such as the Matthew Burrows House on Sixteenth Avenue East and First Street and the Ellery House on Twenty-first Avenue East, between Superior Street and London Road.

Once you pass Twenty-first Avenue East the houses are still almost all well-maintained single-family homes.

To see the really spectacular mansions, get onto London Road. London Road begins at Eleventh Avenue East as a not very impressive strip of fast-food restaurants, gas stations, liquor stores, and inexpensive motels. It hugs the lake, though you can't always see it because of the commerce and development on both sides of the road.

A startling change takes place, though, once you pass about Twenty-sixth Avenue East. Suddenly you'll see trees again, and wide, shady sidewalks. On the lake side, especially, impressive old homes are tucked back so far from the road you will have a hard time spotting them from the car. This would be a good time to park and walk, or take a bicycle.

For the next thirty blocks—just about all the way to the Lester River—you will pass timbered mansions with tennis courts, fountains, and huge gardens; wooded property rimmed with brick walls and protected by stone lions guarding the front gates.

The most famous of these houses is Glensheen, the Jacobean-style mansion built in 1908 by the Chester A. Congdon family. Congdon, a mining and lumber king, moved his family to Duluth in the

Sinclair Lewis

Another notable mansion in Duluth's East End is the large brick home at 2601 East Second Street. This striking house has thirty rooms, six bathrooms, eight fireplaces, and a bowling alley in the basement. ■ In 1945, during a slump in Duluth's economy, this massive house sold for only $15,000—a shocking $85,000 less than it cost to build. The person who bought it at such a bargain price was Sinclair Lewis, the Nobel-winning writer from Sauk Centre, Minnesota. Lewis had gone on to fame in New York and Paris as the author of *Main Street, Babbitt,* and other books. ■ He came to Duluth in May 1944 and first rented the mansion, staying all summer. He purchased the house in January 1945 and promptly arranged for expensive remodeling. But Lewis ended up living here only a short time—the summers of 1944 and 1945 and the winter of 1945–46—before selling the house and returning East. While he was in Duluth, he researched and wrote *Cass Timberlane* and *Kingsblood Royal.*

1800s and made a fortune on the Iron Range. Glensheen remained in his family until 1977, when Elisabeth, the last Congdon daughter, died. The estate was willed to the University of Minnesota-Duluth, which maintains it and has opened it to tours and private parties.

If you enjoy opulence and tasteful extravagance, you'll want to stop by and wander through the thirty-nine-room mansion. It is a home beyond compare in Duluth, with hand-carved pilasters, Circassian walnut and fumed oak woodwork, high-ceilinged rooms with fireplaces and stained glass windows. In the summer, the tour includes the gardens; the Glensheen grounds run straight down toward the cliffs of Lake Superior and include impressive formal gardens, fountains, and

brick walkways. In the winter, the house is decorated for Christmas with dozens of trees trimmed with antique ornaments, bells, wreaths, and fragrant fir boughs. Children's choirs, harpists, and flutists perform concerts in the hallways, and the air smells of gingersnaps and pine.

The house has a notorious past that you will not learn about on any tour; it isn't considered seemly to mention the fact that two elderly women were murdered here while it was still a private residence. In 1977, Elisabeth Congdon, who lived here alone in her later years, was smothered in her bed with a pillow. Her night nurse, Velma Pietila, was bludgeoned to death on the wide oak stairway with a brass candlestick. Congdon's son-in-law, Roger Caldwell, was convicted of both crimes.

Fish Hatchery

Millions of fish now swimming in area lakes can trace their lineage back to the holding pools at the Lester River hatchery.

The hatchery, with its white gingerbread building near the mouth of the river on London Road, was the first such artificial spawning ground on Lake Superior.

The federal government stepped into Lake Superior's fish breeding business in 1887. At the time, Duluth had weathered a series of booms and busts, and was experiencing the start of a sustained boom that would last for forty years. In the decade of the 1880s, Duluth's population jumped from less than four thousand to more than thirty-three thousand. These newcomers cut a lot of trees and ate a lot of fish.

The Fish Hatchery is listed on the National Register of Historic Places.

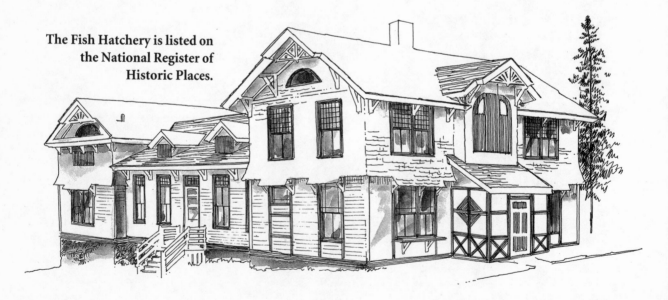

The Fish Hatchery sits on the bank of the Lester River, where the river enters Lake Superior.

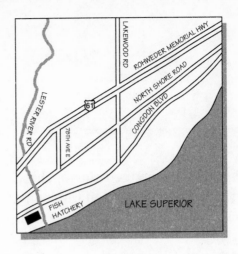

Old photos document the devastation wrought by early clear-cut logging techniques. Early commercial fishing techniques, while tough to record on film, produced similar results. Fishermen at the time used small mesh nets that caught a lot of fish—whitefish among the most prized. However, the nets caught too many undersized young whitefish. *The Lake Superior News* stated at the time that "the wanton destruction of billions of the young every year by the use of small mesh nets gave good ground for the fear of extinction which generally prevailed."

Area fishermen realized their mistakes, and agreed to change the size of the meshing in their nets. At the same time, the Department of the Interior decided to build a hatchery at Lester River.

Eggs, collected by fishermen, grew into fish at the hatchery's holding pools. The federal spawning house expanded the scope of its restocking beyond whitefish. And as the years went by, fingerlings of various species were deposited not only in Lake Superior but in smaller inland lakes throughout the region.

For nearly sixty years, tens of thousands of fish eggs came to maturation at the federal fish hatchery. However, problems with water and egg supply, and the fact that a state-run hatchery had been operating nearby for thirty years, caused the government to phase out the hatchery in 1946. The federal government then donated the wood frame building to the University of Minnesota.

The university packed up the fish raising equipment, and used the building as a storage shed: a shed with one of the best views in town. Today the former hatchery has a different name: Limnological Research Station. Limnology is the study of freshwater lakes, and in recent years researchers have used the hatchery building to study acid rain and mercury levels in water, lake bottoms, and, yes, fish.

Spring ritual

Smelting was once a mighty spring ritual, a festival of revelry and rebirth, a weekend or two in mid-April when thousands of locals gathered at the mouths of the inland rivers to party all night, fill their buckets with fish, and celebrate the end of winter. This rowdy, noisy, and disruptive occasion eventually began to attract hundreds of tourists from the Twin Cities. They made the long drive up Interstate 35 to Duluth while the smelt themselves made the long swim from the middle of Lake Superior to the North Shore rivers.

The 1960s and 1970s were peak years for smelting. Millions of the tiny, squirming silver fish funneled their way from Lake Superior up the inland rivers—the Lester, the French, the Knife. And they were met by thousands of people, once-a-year anglers, who would gather at the mouths of these same rivers with their dipping nets, waders and coolers of beer. Spring had not officially arrived, legend had it, until each successful smelter had grabbed a live, squirming fish in his bare hands and bit its head clean off.

The smelters filled buckets and pickle barrels and coolers by the hundreds with the tiny fish. And, as the raw of the April night set in, they built bonfires and chugged down beer to keep warm. Passersby would see, late on those April midnights, throngs of revelers splashing in the

Fish transplants

The Minnesota Department of Natural Resources has its nets full these days restocking Lake Superior with hatchery-raised fish. More than 750,000 "yearling" fish, 500,000 "fingerlings," and 3,000,000 "fry" are transplanted into Lake Superior every year from Minnesota hatcheries alone.

black waters, triumphantly waving fistfuls of smelt aloft. The eerie red glow of forbidden smoky bonfires lit everything.

Of course, those who lived near the rivers viewed this Bacchanalian rite with great disapproval. Morning after morning, these people found that their fences had been torn down for firewood and their yards had been used as bathrooms. Dead smelt lay scattered in yards and alleys across East Duluth.

Not surprisingly, people complained. Eventually, the city administrators began to listen. Rules were passed, posted, and enforced. The smelters calmed down. Part of the reason for the smelters' obedience might have been that about this same time, the smelt began to disappear, victims of the increase of salmon and trout in the lake.

Smelting has now become a quiet, orderly ritual. In recent years, the smelt have barely bothered to put in an appearance. Smelters, too, are in much shorter supply than they once were. These days, a handful of people show up to dip their nets and vie for a few of the wriggling fish.

But those who live along the riverbanks sleep easier, knowing their yards and porches and fences will survive the ceremony intact.

Pumping Station

Two miles past the Lester River, on the very edge of town, stands a red stone castle. Well, not a castle, really, but a big old building with turrets and round windows and an imposing gate, a building that looks out over the lake as if it is keeping watch over a kingdom.

What it really is doing, though, is something far more prosaic: pumping water.

Duluth's Municipal Pumping Station, on the lake side of Scenic Highway 61, was

The Pumping Station sits on the shore of Lake Superior at the eastern edge of Duluth.

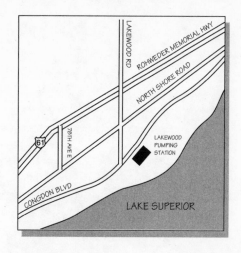

built nearly a century ago. At that time, Duluth had been platted to stretch way up the North Shore. Duluth didn't grow as expected, though, and the elegant pumping station remains on the edge of town, alone, desolate, in a setting of rural, weedy splendor.

It serves as a landmark, of sorts—some people measure their bicycle rides by it, and the thousands of runners who pound past it each June during Grandma's Marathon know that when they've reached the pumping station, they're definitely on the home stretch.

When the station was first built, it housed an enormous coal-fired steam engine—so large that its pistons filled the two-and-a-half-story building. What is now a garage was originally the coal shed, holding the many tons of coal required to fuel the engine. Now most of the space under the building's vaulted roof is empty. The mammoth coal engine has been replaced with quietly humming electric turbines, which push the water from the lake up the steep hills of Duluth to reservoirs and water towers.

And Beyond

In this book you've barely begun to explore Duluth. You've taken a quick scan of the city, from West to East, from Fond du Lac to the North Shore Drive. When you have time why not head back into the neighborhoods you want to explore further. You'll soon discover your own favorite spots—Hartley Field, or Spirit Mountain, or some quirky neighborhood bar and grill. There's nothing more exciting than happening upon a marvelous place on your own and learning to love it.

Discovering a city is a personal adventure, shaped by your own interests and inclinations. History or hiking? Ships or shopping? Fast or fancy food? Art, architecture, antiques? Duluth offers them all. It's up to you to dig in and explore to your liking.

You'll also probably want to head up the North Shore—to see where the curvy old highway takes you. Keep an eye on that big lake and notice what weather and excitement it sends your way.

Go ahead. Get on your bike, or roll down your car windows and feel the moist lake air; smell the fog and the wind. Head up the Shore past all those places with the fascinating names—Silver Cliff and Castle Danger and Little Marais—and see what they're all about.

Then when you're ready, turn your car around and head back into Duluth, once again. The city is waiting for you with landmarks still waiting to be rediscovered.

The publisher would like to thank the following people and institutions for their contributions to *Boomtown Landmarks:* Ethel Hedman for reading an early draft of the manuscript and making suggestions; Donna Carlson, Debbie Swenson, and Jay Peterson of the St. Louis County Heritage & Arts Center for providing further information about the Depot; Bill Graham for information about the trains; the Lake Superior Museum of Transportation for allowing us to use Bruce G. Smith's train illustrations on pages 70 and 71 and streetcar illustration on page 66; Patricia Maus for supplying the architect's drawing of the original Aerial Bridge on page 96, used courtesy of the Northeast Minnesota Historical Center; Pat Labadie for details on the ship canal; Carol Kennedy for copyediting the manuscript and Kathy Prudhomme for proofing it.

The series title *Discover Duluth* is used courtesy of the Duluth Transit Authority.